**David**

**In B**

Methuen Drama

**Published by Methuen Drama 2012**

Methuen Drama, an imprint of Bloomsbury Publishing Plc

1 3 5 7 9 10 8 6 4 2

Methuen Drama
Bloomsbury Publishing Plc
50 Bedford Square
London WC1B 3DP
www.methuendrama.com

ISBN 978 1 408 16482 2

A CIP record for this book is available from the British Library

Available in the USA from Bloomsbury Academic & Professional, 175 Fifth
Avenue /3rd Floor, New York, NY 10010. www.BloomsburyAcademicUSA.com

Typeset by Mark Heslington Ltd, Scarborough, North Yorkshire
Printed and bound in Great Britain by CPI Group (UK) Ltd, Croydon, CR0
4YY

# ROYAL COURT

The Royal Court Theatre presents

# IN BASILDON

## by **DAVID ELDRIDGE**

IN BASILDON was first performed at The Royal Court Jerwood Theatre Downstairs, Sloane Square, on Thursday 16th February 2012.

Principal Sponsor

# IN BASILDON

by David Eldridge

Doreen **Linda Bassett**
Maureen **Ruth Sheen**
Barry **Lee Ross**
Pam **Wendy Nottingham**
Ken **Peter Wight**
Jackie **Debbie Chazen**
Shelley **Jade Williams**
Tom **Max Bennett**
Reverend David Williams **Christian Dixon**
Len **Phil Cornwell**
Young Shelley **Tess Fontaine, Meg Reynolds**

Director **Dominic Cooke**
Designer **Ian MacNeil**
Costume Designer **Nicky Gillibrand**
Lighting Designer **Guy Hoare**
Sound Designer **Paul Arditti**
Casting Director **Amy Ball**
Assistant Director **Caitlin McLeod**
Production Manager **Paul Handley**
Stage Manager **Nafeesah Butt**
Deputy Stage Manager **Ruth Murfitt**
Assistant Stage Manager **Katie Hutcheson**
Dialect Coach **Penny Dyer**
Fight Director **Bret Yount**
Costume Supervisor **Jackie Orton**
Wigs **Carole Hancock**
Set Builders **Miraculous Engineering**
Set Painter **Catherine Goodley**

The Royal Court and Stage Management wish to thank the following for their help with this production: Elaine Henderson-Boyle, Hayley at Hill-Rom, Dr Liza Filby, Debbie Hickey, Sharon Quinn and Anna Tierney.

# THE COMPANY

## DAVID ELDRIDGE (Writer)

FOR THE ROYAL COURT: Incomplete and Random Acts of Kindness, Under the Blue Sky (& Duke of York's).

OTHER THEATRE INCLUDES: Something, Someone, Somewhere, M.A.D., Serving It Up (Bush); The Knot of the Heart (Almeida); Festen (Almeida/Lyric West End/Broadway); The Stock Da'wa, Falling (Hampstead); The Lady from the Sea (Royal Exchange); A Thousand Stars Explode in the Sky (with Robert Holman & Simon Stephens, Lyric Hammersmith); Babylone (Belgrade, Coventry); John Gabriel Borkman, The Wild Duck, Summer Begins (Donmar Warehouse); Market Boy (National); A Week With Tony, Fighting for Breath (Finborough); Thanks Mum (Red Room); Dirty (Stratford East); Cabbage for Tea, Tea, Tea! (Platform 4, Exeter).

TELEVISION INCLUDES: Killers, Our Hidden Lives.

FILM INCLUDES: The Nugget Run.

RADIO INCLUDES: Michael and Me: Stratford, Ilford, Romford and all Stations to Shenfield, Festen, The Picture Man, Like Minded People, The Secret Grief.

AWARDS INCLUDE: 2001 Time Out Live Award for Best New Play in the West End for Under the Blue Sky, 2005 Theatregoers Choice Award for Best New Play for Festen, 2008 Prix Europa Best European Radio Drama for The Picture Man, 2009 Theatregoers Choice Award for Best New Play for Under the Blue Sky.

In April 2012, the Royal Exchange Theatre, Manchester, will premiere his new English version of Strindberg's Miss Julie.

## PAUL ARDITTI (Sound Designer)

FOR THE ROYAL COURT: Jumpy, The Pain and the Itch, A Girl in a Car with a Man, Duck, Plasticine, 4:48 Psychosis, Far Away, Blasted, Via Dolorosa, The Weir, Mojo, Shopping and Fucking, Some Voices, The Kitchen.

OTHER THEATRE INCLUDES: Collaborators, The Veil, One Man Two Guvnors, London Road, Blood and Gifts, Love the Sinner, Never So Good, Happy Now?, Saint Joan, The Revenger's Tragedy, The Year of Magical Thinking (National); The Changeling, The Beauty Queen of Leenane, Been So Long, Member of the Wedding, Vernon God Little, The Respectable Wedding, Generations (Young Vic); Company (Sheffield Crucible); Doctor Dee (Manchester International Festival); The Most Incredible Thing (Sadler's Wells); Billy Elliot the Musical (West End, Broadway, Australia, US Tour); A Ring, A Lamp, A Thing (Royal Opera House); Arabian Nights (RSC); The House of Bernarda Alba (National Theatre of Scotland); When the Rain Stops Falling (Almeida); The Cherry Orchard, The Winter's Tale (The Bridge Project: New York, World Tour & Old Vic); Mary Stuart (Broadway); Under the Blue Sky (West End); Nakamitsu (Gate, London); Herge's Adventures of Tintin (Barbican & West End).

AWARDS INCLUDE: 2009 Tony Award, 2009 Drama Desk Award, 2009 BroadwayWorld.com Fans' Choice Award, 2006 Olivier Award for Billy Elliot the Musical; 2008 Olivier Award for Saint Joan; 2005 Evening Standard Award for Festen; 2005 Drama Desk Award for The Pillowman; 1993 Olivier Award for Four Baboons Adoring the Sun.

www.paularditti.com

## LINDA BASSETT (Doreen)

FOR THE ROYAL COURT: Wastwater, The Stone, Lucky Dog, Far Away (& Albery); East Is East (with Tamasha Theatre Company & Birmingham Rep & Stratford East/Duke of York's); The Recruiting Officer, Our Country's Good (& Garrick); Serious Money (& Wyndhams & Public, NY); Aunt Dan and Lemon (& Public); Abel's Sister, Fen (with Joint Stock & UK tour & Public, NY).

OTHER THEATRE INCLUDES: The Road to Mecca (Arcola); A Winter's Tale, Pericles, Henry IV Parts I & II, The Theban Plays, Artists and Admirers (RSC); Phaedra (Donmar); Hortensia & the Museum of Dreams

(Finborough); Love Me Tonight, The Awakening (Hampstead); Richard III, The Taming of the Shrew (Globe); John Gabriel Borkman (ETT); Out in the Open (Birmingham/Hampstead); Five Kinds of Silence (Lyric Hammersmith); The Dove (Croydon Warehouse); The Triumph of Love (Almeida/UK Tour); The Clearing (Bush); Schism in England, Juno and the Paycock, A Place with the Pigs (National); The Seagull (Liverpool Playhouse); George Dandin, Medea, Woyceck, Bald Prima Donna, The Cherry Orchard (Leicester Haymarket/Liverpool Playhouse/Almeida); Belgrade T.I.E. Team (Coventry); Interplay (Leeds).

TELEVISION INCLUDES: Grandma's House, Lark Rise to Candleford, Sense and Sensibility, The Brief, This Little Life, Our Mutual Friend, Far From the Madding Crowd, Christmas, A Touch of Frost, A Small Dance, No Bananas, Newshounds, A Village Affair, Bramwell, Loved Up, Cold Light of Day, Frank Stubbs Promotes, Skallagrig.

FILM INCLUDES: Effie, West Is West, Cass, The Reader, Separate Lies, Calendar Girls, The Hours, The Martins, East Is East, Beautiful People, Oscar and Lucinda, Waiting for the Moon.

AWARDS INCLUDE: 2004 TMA Best Actress Award for Lucky Dog, 2001 Clarence Derwent Best Actress in a Supporting Role Award for Far Away, 1999 Best Actress Award Semana Internacional de Cine Valladolid España for East Is East.

## MAX BENNETT (Tom)

THEATRE INCLUDES: Luise Miller (Donmar); A Midsummer Night's Dream (Headlong); Fabrication [Affabulazione] (Print Room); Danton's Death (National); Mrs Warren's Profession (West End/UK tour); Measure for Measure (UK Tour); Waste (Almeida); Romeo and Juliet (Theatre of Memory at Middle Temple Hall); Thyestes (BAC); Finisterre (Theatre 503); The Herbal Bed (Salisbury Playhouse).

FILM INCLUDES: Anna Karenina, The Sweeney, The Numbers Station, The Duchess, 99 Francs.

## DEBBIE CHAZEN (Jackie)

FOR THE ROYAL COURT: The Girlfriend Experience (with Drum Theatre, Plymouth & Young Vic).

OTHER THEATRE INCLUDES: Calendar Girls (Noël Coward/UK tour); Where's My Seat? (Bush); Cinderella (Old Vic); The Cherry Orchard (Crucible); Dick Whittington (Barbican); Crooked (Bush); Aladdin (Bristol Old Vic); A Prayer for Owen Meany (National); Mother Clap's Molly House (National/Aldwych); A Midsummer Night's Dream (Albery); The Rise and Fall of Little Voice (Salisbury Playhouse); Frogs (Nottingham Playhouse); The Knife (National Studio).

TELEVISION INCLUDES: Coronation Street, White Van Man, Doctors, We Are Klang, Psychoville, The Wall, Midsomer Murders, The Eejits, Doctor Who, The Clinic, Tittybangbang, Doc Martin, Doctors, The Bill, EastEnders, Cynthia, Murder in Suburbia, Mile High, The Smoking Room, Mine All Mine, Grass, Holby City, Gimme Gimme Gimme, The Estate Agents, Nicholas Nickleby, Casualty, Lucy Sullivan is Getting Married, A Christmas Carol, Ruth Rendell: You Can't Be Too Careful, Tess of the D'Urbervilles, Killer Net, An Unsuitable Job for a Woman, The Lakes.

FILM INCLUDES: The Duel, Feeder, Tooth, Suzie Gold, Beginner's Luck, Topsy-Turvy, Virtuality, The Rendezvous, Barnie Barniche et ses Petites Contrariétés.

RADIO INCLUDES: Dinner Ladies, The Very World of Milton Jones, Giles Wemmbley-Hogg Goes Off, Electric Ink.

## DOMINIC COOKE (Director)

FOR THE ROYAL COURT: Chicken Soup with Barley, Clybourne Park (& Wyndham's), Aunt Dan & Lemon, The Fever, Seven Jewish Children, Wig Out!, Now or Later, War & Peace/Fear & Misery, Rhinoceros, The Pain and the Itch, Other People, Fireface, Spinning into Butter, Redundant, Fucking Games, Plasticine, The People Are Friendly, This is a Chair, Identical Twins.

OTHER THEATRE INCLUDES: The Comedy of Errors (National); Arabian Nights, Pericles, The Winter's Tale, The Crucible, Postcards from America, As You Like It, Macbeth, Cymbeline, The Malcontent (RSC); By the Bog of Cats (Wyndham's); The Eccentricities of a Nightingale (Gate, Dublin); Arabian Nights (Young Vic/UK & World tours/New Victory Theatre, New York); The Weavers, Hunting Scenes from Lower Bavaria (Gate); The Bullet (Donmar); Afore Night Come, Entertaining Mr Sloane (Clwyd); The

Importance of Being Earnest (Atlantic Theatre Festival, Canada); Caravan (National Theatre of Norway); My Mother Said I Never Should (Oxford Stage Co./Young Vic); Kiss of the Spider Woman (Bolton Octagon); Of Mice and Men (Nottingham Playhouse); Autogeddon (Assembly Rooms).

OPERA INCLUDES: The Magic Flute (WNO); I Capuleti E I Montecchi, La Bohème (Grange Park Opera).

AWARDS INCLUDE: Olivier Awards for Best Director and Best Revival for The Crucible; TMA Award for Arabian Nights; Fringe First Award for Autogeddon.

Dominic was Associate Director of the Royal Court 1999–2002, Associate Director of RSC 2002–2006 & Assistant Director RSC 1992–1993.

Dominic is Artistic Director of the Royal Court.

## PHIL CORNWELL (Len)

FOR THE ROYAL COURT: The Village Bike.

OTHER THEATRE INCLUDES: The Birthday Party, Look Back in Anger (ESTA); I Could Never Be Your Woman (Could Never Ltd.); Journey's End (Background); Outbreak of God in Area 9 (Young Vic); Small Expectations (Elizabeth Hall); Wasp 05 (Jelly Roll Prods); A View from the Bridge (Bankside).

TELEVISION INCLUDES: The Starlings, Hustle, Skins, Game Over, Harry and Paul, The Legend of Dick and Dom, Missing, Omid 'B', Hotel Trubble, Dani's House, Doctor Who, Headcases, MI High, Phoo Action, The Shadow in the North, Dead Ringers, The Comic Strip Presents, Dunkirk, I'm Alan Partridge, The Bill, Holby City, Murder in Mind, Clocking Off, Happiness, World of Pub, Stella Street, Fun at the Funeral Parlour, Sunburn, Gormenghast, Only Fools and Horses, Trial and Retribution III, Big Train.

FILM INCLUDES: Cockneys vs Zombies, Made in Dagenham, Lady Godiva: Back in the Saddle, I Could Never Be Your Woman, Scoop, Colour Me Kubrick, Chromophobia, Churchill: The Hollywood Years, Large, Blood, Out of Depth, Stella Street The Movie.

RADIO INCLUDES: Polly Oaks, The Cornwell Estate, 28 Acts in 28 Minutes, And This Is Them, Blue Jam III, Cinema Scrapbook, First Impressions, Front Row, King of the Road, Lenin of the Rovers, Loose Ends, Mango, Night Cap, Overtime, Remember Live Aid, Spoilsports, The Comedy Controller, The Day the Music Died, The Pits, Watching with Monkey, Weekending.

## CHRISTIAN DIXON (Reverend David Williams)

THEATRE INCLUDES: Mogadishu (Royal Exchange); Burn My Heart (Trestle Theatre Co.); Shakespeare's Monologues (Off the Page Theatre Co.); The Little Foxes (Donmar); The Giant's Baby (Polka); Much Ado About Nothing (Principle Theatre Co.); Macbeth (Orange Tree); The Tempest (Young Shakespeare Co.); The Park/A Midsummer Night's Dream (Old Vic); Kissing the Pope, The Plantagenets, The Plain Dealer (RSC); Macbeth (Cheek by Jowl).

TELEVISION INCLUDES: Brum, Escape from Kampala.

FILM INCLUDES: European Psycho, Fight for Your Life, Rory & Clive, Pat.

## TESS FONTAINE (Young Shelley)

TELEVISION INCLUDES: Great Expectations.

In Basildon is Tess's professional stage debut.

## NICKY GILLIBRAND (Costume Designer)

THEATRE INCLUDES: Hamlet, The Government Inspector, Annie Get Your Gun, The Good Soul of Szechuan, Vernon God Little (Young Vic); King Lear (Liverpool Playhouse/Everyman/Young Vic); Billy Elliot (West End/Broadway/Chicago/Australia); The Tempest, A Midsummer Night's Dream (RSC); The Seagull, Tales from Vienna Woods (National).

OPERA INCLUDES: Il Trittico, Anna Nicole, The Gambler, L'Heure Espagnole/Gianni Schicchi, Lady Macbeth of Mtsensk (Royal Opera); Queen of Spades (Royal Opera/Naples/Geneva); Rusalka (Copenhagen); The Fiery Angel (Brussels); The Midsummer Marriage (Munich); Miserly Knight, Gianni Schicchi, Flight (Glyndebourne); La Traviata, Hansel and Gretel, Don Carlos and Wozzeck (Opera North); War and Peace (Paris); Cavalleria Rusticana/Pagliacci, Pelléas and Mélisande, Don Giovanni (ENO).

AWARDS INCLUDE: 2003 Prague Quadrennial Gold Medal for Best Costume Design for A Midsummer Night's Dream.

## GUY HOARE (Lighting Designer)

THEATRE INCLUDES: Be Near Me, Serenading Louie (Donmar); A Delicate Balance, Waste (Almeida); Othello (West End); And No More Shall We Part (Hampstead); Electra (The Gate); Peter Pan (NTS); Future Proof (Traverse); Faith Healer (Bristol Old Vic); A Christmas Carol (Birmingham Rep); Annie, As You Like It, Macbeth (West Yorkshire Playhouse); Kes (Liverpool Playhouse); Amadeus, Assassins, Fen, Far Away (Crucible Theatre, Sheffield); Going Dark (Sound & Fury).

DANCE INCLUDES: The Metamorphosis (ROH2 / Arthur Pita); The Land of Yes, the Land of No (Sydney Dance Company); Square Map of Q4 (Bonachela Dance Company); And Who Shall Come to the Ball? (Candoco); The Lessening of Difference, About Around (bgroup); Mischief (Theatre Rites); Love & War; Sea of Bones (Mark Bruce Company); Frontline; White Space; Second Signal, Shot Flow (Henri Oguike Dance Company); Bruise Blood, Flicker (Shobana Jeyasingh Dance Company).

OPERA INCLUDES: The Cunning Little Vixen (National Theatre, Brno); La Clemenza di Tito, Gianni Schicchi, Il Tabarro, Fantastic Mr Fox, Promised End, The Duenna, The Magic Flute, Katya Kabanova, Don Giovanni, Anna Bolena, Susannah, The Seraglio, Eugene Onegin (ETO); The Ring Cycle, Tosca (Longborough Festival Opera).

## IAN MACNEIL (Set Designer)

FOR THE ROYAL COURT: Far Away (& Albery & New York Theatre Workshop), Via Dolorosa (& Broadway & West End), This is a Chair, Body Talk, The Editing Process, Death and the Maiden (& UK Tour), Plasticine and A Number.

OTHER THEATRE INCLUDES: Peribanez, Afore Night Come, Vernon God Little (Young Vic); Albert Speer, Machinal (RNT); An Inspector Calls (RNT/West End/Broadway/Int. Tour); The Ingolstadt Plays, Figaro Gets Divorced, Jerker (Gate); The Picture of Dorian Gray (Lyric, Hammersmith); Enter Achilles, Bound to Please (DV8); Festen (Almeida/West End/Broadway); Billy Elliot the Musical (West End/Broadway/Australia/US Tour); Tintin (Barbican/Playhouse).

OPERA INCLUDES: Don Giovani, Tristan and Isolde, Der Freischutz (ENO); Medea (Opera North); Ariodante (ENO, WNO, Houston Grand Opera); La Traviata (Paris Opera); Il Ritorno d'Ulisse in Patria (Munich Opera); Ulysses (WNO).

TELEVISION AND FILM INCLUDES: Winterreise, Eight, Pet Shop Boys World Tour 2000 & 2002.

AWARDS INCLUDE: 2010 Olivier Award for Best Opera for Tristan and Isolde, 2004 Evening Standard Award for Best Designer for Festen, 2002 Evening Standard Award for Best Designer for Plasticine and A Number, 1993 Critics Circle Award for Best Design for Machinal, 1992 Critics Circle Award for Best Design for An Inspector Calls, 1992 Olivier Award for Best Design for An Inspector Calls.

## CAITLIN MCLEOD (Assistant Director)

AS ASSISTANT DIRECTOR FOR THE ROYAL COURT: Haunted Child.

OTHER THEATRE DIRECTION INCLUDES: And I And Silence, Northern Star (Finborough); Slaughter City (RSC, Rehearsed reading); The Lady's Not for Burning, Elephant's Graveyard (Warwick Arts Centre Studio); Seven Jewish Children (Capital Centre).

OTHER ASSISTANT DIRECTION INCLUDES: Hamlet (Globe); The Talented Mr Ripley (Northampton Theatre Royal); Touched (North Wall Theatre, Oxford).

Caitlin is the Trainee Director at the Royal Court.

## WENDY NOTTINGHAM (Pam)

FOR THE ROYAL COURT: The York Realist (with English Touring Theatre/UK Tour & Strand); The Madness of Esme and Shaz, Ambulance.

OTHER THEATRE INCLUDES: Grief, The Shaughraun, The Voysey Inheritance (National); Fen (Finborough); Blithe Spirit (Manchester Royal Exchange); Natural Selection (Theatre 503); Stoopud Fucken Animals (Traverse); Total Eclipse (Menier); Cloud Nine (Crucible); Abigail's Party

(Hampstead/Ambassadors); Rupert Street Lonely Hearts Club (Criterion); It's a Great Big Shame! (Stratford East); The Way of the World (Lyric Hammersmith); Jane Eyre (Leeds Playhouse); The Crucible (Young Vic Studio).

TELEVISION INCLUDES: Crimson Petal and the White, Casualty, Victoria Wood's Christmas Special, Getting On, Spooks, Silent Witness, Lewis, Kingdom, The Bill, Miss Marple, House Wife 49, Extras, The Rise and Fall of Rome, The Golden Hour, Kiss Me Kate, Extremely Dangerous, People Like Us, The People Principle, McCallum, A Wing and a Prayer, The Peter Principle, The Pale Horse, The Sculptress, Bliss, The Vet, Bramwell, The Wimbledon Poisoner, Kinsey, Shrinks, A Very Peculiar Practice, What's Got into You, Tumbledown, Precious Bane, The Short and Curlies.

FILM INCLUDES: Atonement, Bigga than Ben, Notes on a Scandal, Babel, Vera Drake, Topsy-Turvy, Secret and Lies, The Short and Curlies.

## MEG REYNOLDS (Young Shelley)

In Basildon is Megan's professional acting debut.

## LEE ROSS (Barry)

FOR THE ROYAL COURT: Country Music, The Lights, Some Voices, Hammett's Apprentice, Children's Day.

OTHER THEATRE INCLUDES: Birdsong (Comedy); Marine Parade (Brighton Festival); Whipping It Up (Bush & West End); M.A.D., Christmas (Bush); The Neighbour (National); Spookhouse (Hampstead); Bugsy Malone (Her Majesty's).

TELEVISION INCLUDES: Open Doors: Love in a Mist, Titanic, Midsomer Murders, Dr Who, Coming Up – Geronimo, Ashes to Ashes, The Bill, The Scum Also Rises, Moses Jones, Robin Hood, The Catherine Tate Show, Jericho, Dunkirk, Hustle, Waking the Dead, Playing the Field, Trial & Retribution, Shine On Harvey Moon, Thief Takers, SAB, The Negotiator, 99-1, Between the Lines, The Guilty, Shrinks, Work, Shoot the Revolution, Amongst Barbarians, Press Gang, Life on Mars.

FILM INCLUDES: Centurion, Goal, Secret and Lies, Dockers, Dreaming of Joseph Lees, Rogue Trader, Vigo, Metroland, Island on Bird Street, Hard Men, The English Patient, I.D., The Crane, Life's a Gas, Sweet Nothing, Buddy's Song.

## RUTH SHEEN (Maureen)

FOR THE ROYAL COURT: Stoning Mary.

OTHER THEATRE INCLUDES: Leaves of Glass, An Oak Tree (Soho); Market Boy (National); It's a Great Big Shame, Red Riding Hood (Stratford East); Othello (German tour); Dreamer, Children for Sale, Short Circuit Popeye (Half Moon); Kept In/Kept Out (Avon touring); Twelfth Night (E15); Crime of the Century (Wolsey); Ten Tiny Fingers (Library); The Home Service (Bloomsbury/Edinburgh Fest.); As You Like It (Ludlow Festival).

TELEVISION INCLUDES: Accused, Silent Witness, Fanny Hill, The Spastic King, A Class Apart, Vital Signs, The English Harem, Doc Martin, Footprints in the Snow, Imagine Me and You, 20,000 Streets Under the Sky, Miss Marple, White Teeth, Plain Jane, Lorna Doone, Never Never, Don Quixote, Berkeley Square, Tom Jones, Cracker, Holding On, Bramwell, Sin Bin, Casualty, Downtown Lagos, Clubland, A Fatal Inversion, Ghostwatch, Crossing the Border, London's Burning, The Bill, King and Castle, Fry and Laurie, Making Out, Night Voice.

FILM INCLUDES: Welcome to the Punch, Another Year, Heartless, The Hardest Part, Run Fat Boy Run, Vera Drake, Vanity Fair, Cheeky, All or Nothing, Bait, Secrets and Lies, Virtual Sexuality, Young Poisoners Handbook, When Pigs Fly, Little Dorrit, High Hopes, The Angry Earth.

AWARDS INCLUDES: 1989 European Film Award for Best Actress for High Hopes.

## PETER WIGHT (Ken)

FOR THE ROYAL COURT: The Seagull (& Broadway); Mouth to Mouth, Face to the Wall, Not a Game for Boys.

OTHER THEATRE INCLUDES: Otherwise Engaged (Criterion); Ivanov, Sleep with Me, Murmuring Judges, Arturo Ui, Black Snow, Waiting for Godot (National); The Spanish Tragedy, Much Ado About Nothing, Barbarians, A Clockwork Orange, Hamlet (RSC); The Caretaker (Globe Theatre, Warsaw); Edward II (Manchester Royal Exchange); Dearly Beloved, Grace (Hampstead); A State of Affairs, Othello, Comedia, Progress (Lyric, Hammersmith); The Seagull (UK tour & Lyric, Hammersmith); Chekhov's Women (Lyric, West End); Julius Caesar (Riverside); A Passion in Six Days, A Midsummer Night's Dream, The Nest (Crucible, Sheffield); King Lear, The Three Sisters (Birmingham Rep.), The Seagull (Shared Experience); Hard To Get (Traverse), Sudlow's Dawn.

TELEVISION INCLUDES: Hit and Miss, Public Enemies, Case Sensitive, Titanic, Money, Monday Monday, Boy Meets Girl, 10 Days to War, Party Animals, Dalziel and Pascoe, Eastenders, Persuasion, Fantabulosa, Waking the Dead, Murder Prevention, Early Doors I & II, Silent Witness, Murphy's Law, Uncle Adolf, Brides in the Bath, Charles II, 40 Something, Midsomer Murders, The Second Coming, Care, Active Defence, The Project, The Blind Date, The Passion, Our Mutual Friend, Jane Eyre, Wokenwell, Out of the Blue, Anna Lee, Hearts and Minds, Meat, Devil's Advocate, Speaking in Tongues, Codename Kyril, Exclusive Yarns, Save Your Kisses, Yesterday's Dreams.

FILM INCLUDES: Another Year, Kontiki, Hard Boiled Sweets, Ghosted, Cass, Womb, Atonement, Hot Fuzz, Lassie, Babel, Pride and Prejudice, Vera Drake, The Statement, 3 Blind Mice, The Gathering, Lucky Break, The Fourth Angel, The Shiner, The Return of the Native, Personal Services, Fairy Tale: A True Story, Meantime, Naked, Secrets and Lies.

## JADE WILLIAMS (Shelley)

THEATRE INCLUDES: Doctor Faustus, The God of Soho, Henry IV Part I & II, Bedlam, As You Like It, A New World (Globe); Romeo and Juliet (Globe/UK tour); Palace of the End (Arcola); Shraddha, Piranha Heights (Soho); Chatroom/Citizenship (National/Hong Kong Arts Festival); Market Boy (National); I Like Mine with a Kiss (Bush); The Little Prince (Hampstead); 'Low Dat (Birmingham Rep.).

TELEVISION INCLUDES: DCI Banks, Holby City, EastEnders, Judge John Deed, The Canterbury Tales, William & Mary, Bad Girls, Being April, Doctors, Mile High, Serious & Organised, The Bill, Lloyd & Hill, Casualty, Plotlands, Blackhearts in Battersea.

FILM INCLUDES: Anne Frank, Life & Lyrics, Hush Your Mouth.

RADIO INCLUDES: The Gate of Angels, Marnie, Arcadia, Five Wedding Dresses – The Rescue, Needle, The Chronicles of Narnia, Secrets, The Third Trial, The Mother of…, The Family Man, The Birds, What Is She Doing Here?, The Day the Planes Came, Westway.

# THE ENGLISH STAGE COMPANY
# AT THE ROYAL COURT THEATRE

*'For me the theatre is really a religion or way of life. You must decide what you feel the world is about and what you want to say about it, so that everything in the theatre you work in is saying the same thing ... A theatre must have a recognisable attitude. It will have one, whether you like it or not.'*

George Devine, first Artistic Director of the English Stage Company: notes for an unwritten book

photo: Stephen Cummiskey

As Britain's leading national company dedicated to new work, the Royal Court Theatre produces new plays of the highest quality, working with writers from all backgrounds, and addressing the problems and possibilities of our time.

'The Royal Court has been at the centre of British cultural life for the past 50 years, an engine room for new writing and constantly transforming the theatrical culture.' Stephen Daldry

Since its foundation in 1956, the Royal Court has presented premieres by almost every leading contemporary British playwright, from John Osborne's *Look Back in Anger* to Caryl Churchill's *A Number* and Tom Stoppard's *Rock 'n' Roll*. Just some of the other writers to have chosen the Royal Court to premiere their work include Edward Albee, John Arden, Richard Bean, Samuel Beckett, Edward Bond, Leo Butler, Jez Butterworth, Martin Crimp, Ariel Dorfman, Stella Feehily, Christopher Hampton, David Hare, Eugène Ionesco, Ann Jellicoe, Terry Johnson, Sarah Kane, David Mamet, Martin McDonagh, Conor McPherson, Joe Penhall, Lucy Prebble, Mark Ravenhill, Simon Stephens, Wole Soyinka, Polly Stenham, David Storey, debbie tucker green, Arnold Wesker and Roy Williams.

'It is risky to miss a production there.' *Financial Times*

In addition to its full-scale productions, the Royal Court also facilitates international work at a grass roots level, developing exchanges which bring young writers to Britain and sending British writers, actors and directors to work with artists around the world. The research and play development arm of the Royal Court Theatre, The Studio, finds the most exciting and diverse range of new voices in the UK. The Studio runs playwriting groups including the Young Writers Programme, Critical Mass for black, Asian and minority ethnic writers and the biennial Young Writers Festival. For further information, go to www.royalcourttheatre.com/playwriting/the-studio.

'Yes, the Royal Court is on a roll. Yes, Dominic Cooke has just the genius and kick that this venue needs ... It's fist-bitingly exciting.' *Independent*

# ROYAL COURT SUPPORTERS

The Royal Court is able to offer its unique playwriting and audience development programmes because of significant and longstanding partnerships with the organisations that support it.

Coutts is the Principal Sponsor of the Royal Court. The Genesis Foundation supports the Royal Court's work with international playwrights. Theatre Local is sponsored by Bloomberg. The Jerwood Charitable Foundation supports new plays by playwrights through the Jerwood New Playwrights series. Over the past ten years the BBC has supported the Gerald Chapman Fund for directors.

The Harold Pinter Playwright's Award is given annually by his widow, Lady Antonia Fraser, to support a new commission at the Royal Court.

Supported by
**ARTS COUNCIL ENGLAND**

**Jerwood Theatre Downstairs**
Tickets £28, £20, £12
Mondays all seats £10

27 Apr–2 Jun
# love love love
**by Mike Bartlett**
**co-production with Paines Plough**
**in association with Drum Theatre Plymouth**

22 Jun–4 Aug
# birthday
**by Joe Penhall**

---

**Jerwood Theatre Upstairs**
Tickets £20 Mondays all seats £10

26 Apr–26 May
# belong
**by Bola Agbaje**
**co-production with Tiata Fahodzi**

1–30 Jun
# the witness
**by Vivienne Franzmann**

---

**Young Writers Festival 2012**
Tickets £20 Mondays all seats £10

23 Feb–17 Mar
# goodbye to all that
**by Luke Norris**

22 Mar–14 Apr
# vera vera vera
**by Hayley Squires**

Extra events as part of the **Young Writers Festival**
will include spoken word, writing workshops and
music. Visit our website for more information.

Principal Sponsor
*Coutts*

# 020 7565 5000
## www.royalcourttheatre.com

Supported by
**ARTS COUNCIL
ENGLAND**

# In Basildon

*For Mum and Dad,*
*for all the love and the hope*

*We brought nothing in to the world; for that matter we cannot take anything with us when we leave, but if we have food and covering we may rest content. Those who want to be rich fall into temptation and snares and many foolish, harmful desires which plunge men into ruin and perdition. The love of money is the root of all evil things, and there are some who in reaching for it have wandered from the faith and spiked themselves on many thorny griefs.*

(From the First Letter of Paul to Timothy)

*The picture I have drawn is a harsh one, yet my tone is not one of disgust – nor should it be in the presentation of the plays. I am at one with these people: it is only that I am annoyed, with them and myself.*

(From Arnold Wesker's note to actors and producers of *Roots)*

## Characters

**Doreen**
**Maureen**
**Barry**
**Pam**
**Ken**
**Jackie**
**Shelley**
**Tom**
**Reverend David Williams**
**Len**

# *Act One*

*Late November 2010.*

*A large living room in a semi-detached house in Basildon.*

*The dining table has been pushed against one wall, the sofa against another wall, so there is room for a bed in the room.*

**Len**, *60, is in the bed. He is close to death.*

*With him is his sister* **Doreen**, *55, and her son* **Barry**, *37.*

*Also there is* **Ken**, *75.*

*They all look at* **Len**, *they can't take their eyes off of him. Silence.*

**Maureen**, **Len***'s other sister, 50, enters. Silence.*

**Doreen**   Hello Maureen.

*Silence.*

**Maureen**   Hello Doreen.

*She looks past* **Doreen** *and goes to* **Len**. *Silence.*

**Maureen**   Lenny?

*Silence.*

**Maureen**   Len? Its Maureen. I'm here Len.

**Doreen**   He can't hear you Maureen. You're too late.

*Silence.*

**Maureen**   He can hear me can't you Len? You can hear me.

**Doreen**   You should have been here days ago.

**Maureen**   Len.

*Tears prick her eyes and she blinks, and wipes them away. Silence.*

**Barry**   Thanks for coming Maur.

*Silence.*

**Doreen**   Maur.

**Maureen** *completely ignores her sister. Silence.*

**Maureen**    Will you tell your mother I've had nothing to say to her for nigh on twenty year and I'm here for Len. I'm not here for her. Tell your mother Barry, I wish it was her. That's all I feel towards her.

*Silence.*

**Barry**    Maur.

**Maureen**    Don't Maur me Barry.

**Barry**    I ain't having this.

**Doreen**    She's always been the same. But let's not have a scene Maur. Not tonight. There's not much time darling.

*She stands and looks at* **Maureen** *asserting herself. Silence.*

**Pam**, *55, enters.*

**Pam**    Would anyone like a drink? It's Maureen isn't it? Would you like a drink? Would you like a cup of tea? I've got a kettle on. Slice of angel cake?

**Maureen**    No.

**Doreen**    Later Pam.

**Pam** *notices* **Doreen** *glaring at her.* **Pam** *leaves. Silence.*

**Maureen**    Who's she?

**Barry**    Pam next door.

*Silence.*

**Ken**    Pain in the arse if you ask me.

**Barry**    She's got a good heart.

**Ken**    She's got a lovely couple of raspberries on her an'all but she's still an Alka-Seltzer in the arse-hole.

**Barry**    Trap it Ken.

**Ken**    Len can't hear.

**Barry**  I don't care.

**Ken**  Anyway I'll put a smile on his face.

**Barry**  Shut up Ken.

**Ken**  I've always put a smile on his face. Do you remember me Maureen?

**Maureen**  Course I do.

**Ken**  Ken.

**Maureen**  I remember you Ken. I remember you with my Shelley on your knee.

**Ken**  How's your girl?

**Maureen**  Shelley?

**Ken**  How's your Shelley?

**Maureen**  She's doing well for herself Ken.

**Ken**  Is she?

**Maureen**  She's a teacher.

**Ken**  Got a fella has she?

**Maureen**  Yer she's got a fella.

**Ken**  I bet she's a Bobby Dazzler if she take's after you.

**Maureen** *laughs.* **Doreen** *tuts.*

**Barry**  Ken.

**Ken**  What son?

**Barry**  Turn it down will you?

**Ken**  What?

**Barry**  Try and have a sense of decorum eh mate?

**Ken**  Len wanted me here.

**Barry**  So you say.

**Ken**   Listen big bollocks.

**Barry**   Don't start Ken. Please. This is what I'm saying.

**Ken**   Listen son for once in your life let me educate you.

**Barry**   Here we go.

**Ken**   Listen.

**Barry**   Go on.

**Ken**   Listen.

**Barry**   Go on get it over with. Please Ken. I'm dying here.

*Silence.*

**Ken**   I'm telling you Len wanted me here.

**Barry**   This is hard enough as it is.

**Ken**   I know son, I know.

**Barry**   For three days now you've sat in that chair and you've been in my ear.

**Ken**   What?

**Barry**   We're near the end of the road now. You heard what the nurse said. Say goodbye. I know he loved you. But say goodbye and leave us to it. I know you're his best mate and everything but enough's enough. It's time for the family.

**Ken**   'To the bitter end' he said. Go on, go and find the nurse. It's in his End of Life Plan. Its in Len's notes. Go on you ask her. 'Ken: To the bitter end.' That's what it says. He made her write it down. Exactly them words.

**Barry**   I bet it fucking is an'all.

**Ken**   It fucking is mate.

**Barry**   Go home.

**Ken**   He wanted me here. Do you think he wanted to be left alone with you lot bickering?

**Maureen** *and* **Doreen** *glare at* **Ken**. *Silence.*

**Barry**  It's like a disease and it gets worse the older he gets. The shit just pours out of his mouth.

**Ken**  You'll always be the plumber's mate to me Barry.

**Barry**  If you don't put a sock in it Uncle Len won't be the first one to meet his maker tonight.

**Doreen**  Shut up the pair of you. And you Barry? If there was a great big pile of shit right in front of your face you'd still walk in it.

*Silence.*

**Doreen**  And, I don't know what you're talking about Ken.

**Ken**  What?

**Doreen**  His End of Life Plan's about his palliative care.

**Ken**  I mark you right Dor. But it's not the only thing he wanted sorted. There's things he wanted for tonight.

**Doreen**  I know what my brother wants.

**Ken**  Do you?

**Doreen**  Yes darling I do.

**Ken**  I'm sorry Dor you don't know darling.

**Barry**  Don't push your luck Ken.

**Doreen**  I think Barry's right Ken. We all think the world of yer. You know we all do.

*Silence.*

**Doreen**  But I think you should go home darling. Thanks for coming. We'll let you know.

*Silence.*

**Ken**  Go and ask the nurse.

**Doreen**  I don't need to ask the nurse Ken.

**Ken**  Why do you think he did it?

**Doreen**    You tell me Ken?

**Ken**    Because he didn't want you lot fighting like cat and dog while he's lying there fighting for his life that's why.

*Silence.*

**Maureen**    How do you know?

**Ken**    Because I was holding his hand when the Macmillan nurse wrote down what he wanted.

*He gets caught. Wipes his eyes. Silence.*

**Barry** *wipes his eyes, which sets off* **Doreen** *who wipes her eyes. Silence.*

**Ken**    You see it goes back a long way with Len and me. Your Uncle Len always liked me because I'm authentic Basildon.

**Barry**    I've heard it all now.

**Ken**    I am.

**Barry**    Go on.

**Ken**    I am. The trouble with you Barry is you're good at opening your mouth but you're no good at opening your ears.

**Pam** *enters.*

**Pam**    Brandy any one? Brandy? Anyone fancy a tot?

**Doreen**    We'll give you a shout Pam darling if there's anything you can do. All right?

**Pam**    Are you saying you want me to go home?

**Doreen**    No.

**Pam**    Because if I'm not wanted I'll go home. My Terry's waiting for his spam, egg and chips. I'm only next door. All you've got to do is pick up the phone. We don't even have to speak. You probably won't want to speak. Just let it ring twice and I'll know it's you. The kettle's boiled and the glasses are on the nice tray.

**Doreen** Yes Pam.

**Barry** *puts his head in his hands.* **Pam** *glances at* **Len** *lying in his bed.*

**Pam** Ah look at him poor sod. I'd have given my right arm for a man like your Len.

*She turns on her heel and leaves quickly. Silence.*

**Maureen** *looks at* **Ken** *and then* **Barry** *for an explanation.*

**Doreen** Will you tell your Auntie Maureen, Pam next door was always sweet on our Lenny. I know she's a pain in the arse but she's got a good heart. She wants to be here and Len never had no-one of his own.

**Barry** Don't you start.

**Maureen** And why was your Uncle Len on his own Barry? Eh?

*Silence.*

**Ken** You see I'm authentic Basildon. If there was a Basildon stick of rock. In a manner of speaking. And I was that stick of rock. I would have Basildon spelled right down me insides. B–A–S–I–L–D–O–N.

**Barry** Here he can spell. Look at that mum. Look. Look at that Auntie Maureen. What a marvel.

*He takes out his iPhone which he looks at.*

**Ken** I hope that's switched off.

**Barry** Is yours switched off?

**Ken** *takes out his old Nokia phone and ensures it is switched off.* **Barry** *continues playing with his iPhone.*

**Barry** Here Ken, how long does it take to wind that up in the morning?

**Ken** Oh I've got a charger for it.

**Barry** *kills himself laughing and* **Ken** *shakes his head and waves his phone in the air.*

**Ken**    'We have the technology.'

**Barry**    What's that from?

**Ken**    *The Six Million Dollar Man*.

**Barry**    Did that have Lee Majors?

**Ken**    That's it.

**Barry**    I remember that. They showed the repeats when I was a kid. D'you remember the original *Flash Gordon*?

**Ken**    The black and white one?

**Barry**    Yeah. I can remember watching it with Uncle Len.

**Ken**    How's he doing poppet?

**Maureen**    He's fine.

**Doreen**    She wouldn't know Ken. She's not been here. Not like us.

*She glares at her sister but* **Maureen** *refuses to look at her. Silence.*

**Barry**    So come on Ken give it to me. Authentic Basildon. I am all ears.

**Ken**    No it's all right I'll leave it.

**Barry**    Go on mate. Stick of rock. You've got me where you want me.

**Ken**    No you're taking the piss.

**Barry**    Stick of rock? More like a tube of Colgate. Here Ken you still on Facebook?

**Ken**    Don't know what the fuss is all about.

**Barry**    Nah?

**Ken** I tell you what though that sort from the The Castle Mayne turned up on that Facebook. Poked me. Tacky. Know what I mean?

**Barry** You're like a dog with two dicks.

**Ken** Now what was her name?

**Barry** Ah. Are you having another senior moment Ken?

**Ken** You know we used to call her Kronenbourg.

**Barry** Kronenbourg?

**Ken** She looks sixteen from the back and sixty-four from the front.

*It takes a moment for the penny to drop then* **Barry** *kills himself laughing.* **Maureen** *and* **Doreen** *start to laugh despite themselves. Then* **Maureen** *notices* **Doreen** *is laughing and stops herself. Silence.*

**Ken** Now what was her name? It's gone. We had some laughs didn't we Lenny boy? Eh?

*Silence.*

We had some laughs. You know you can get Viagra for women now Dor?

**Doreen** I'm sure you can Ken.

**Ken** Women have needs.

**Doreen** That's right darling. They do. It's a long time since I've known the feeling of a strong man. I can tell yer.

**Ken** Your mother's making me blush here Barry.

**Doreen** He was always trying to knock on my door Barry.

*She laughs.* **Barry** *looks at his iPhone.* **Maureen** *tuts. Silence.*

**Ken** What's up Barry?

**Barry** You know there's a line Ken.

**Ken** It's why your Uncle Len always liked me. I'm one of life's tryers.

**Barry**   You know you're embarrassing mum with your mouth.

**Ken**   I don't think so. She's worse than me. You're not embarrassed are you Dor?

**Doreen**   Not really Ken, no.

**Ken**   You're not embarrassed are you Maur?

**Maureen**   No Ken, not really.

**Ken**   That's cos your mother and your Auntie Maureen know a sense of humour when they see one Bazza.

**Barry**   Don't fucking call me Bazza. He knows I hate it.

**Ken** *kills himself laughing. Silence.*

**Maureen**   What did Lenny want for the end?

*Silence.*

**Ken**   He said he wanted me here. He said he didn't want misery. He said at the very end he wants us to sing over him.

*Silence.*

**Maureen**   What does he want us to sing?

**Ken**   You know what he wants us to sing darling.

**Maureen** *nods. Silence.*

**Doreen** *stands and makes to leave.*

**Barry**   Mum?

**Doreen** *thinks and then goes. Silence.*

**Barry**   That's you that is.

**Ken**   Barry. Chill out mate. Chill out. You want to get off that estate. You're always stressed. You're always stressing about your van getting nicked. Or your tools getting nicked. You should have got out when they first started re-homing everybody.

**Barry**   Turn the record over. And don't tell me to chill out. Not tonight mate.

*Silence.*

**Ken**   It's just a bit of banter. Keep it light. That's all it is.

*Silence.*

**Maureen**   You enjoying retirement then Ken?

**Ken**   It's all right. I wouldn't say I'm the Six Million Dollar Man but I've got a few quid and I do what I like.

**Maureen** *looks at* **Len**. *Silence.*

**Ken**   I do the odd job when Barry gets stuck just to keep me hand in and the dementia at bay.

**Barry**   It's not helping much is it?

**Ken**   I've got me own spot at the end of the bar in the clubhouse now Maur.

*Silence.*

Has anyone ever told you, you're a handsome woman Maur?

**Maureen**   I bet you say that to everyone.

**Ken**   Au contraire.

**Barry** *coughs loudly.*

**Ken**   What's up Barry d'you want a Fisherman's Friend?

**Barry** *points to* **Len**.

**Barry**   There's a time and a place for trying to knock off Auntie Maureen.

**Maureen** *looks at* **Ken** *and smiles.* **Ken** *winks at her.*

**Ken**   Hey Barry, I thought they were blowing up the flats before Christmas?

**Barry**   I don't know. It's gonna be early next year now. They can't demolish the flats like chimney stacks for some

reason and it took ages to get the last one out. Some
councillor's been moaning about it in *The Recorder*. S'pose he
wants to have his picture taken pushing a big red button.
Like *The Big I Am*. They better do something. They've
boarded the place up now but the security's a joke. They've
got crack-heads and junkies and brasses and God knows
what going in and out of there. It's disgusting.

**Ken**   I remember when they went up. I mean it's hard to
credit it now. But people actually wanted to live in them.
Didn't they Maur? You can give some tower block a fancy
name but a shit-hole's still a shit-hole in my book.

**Barry**   Don't you call it a shit-hole!

**Ken**   You called it a shit-hole! You called it a shit-hole!
You've called it every name under the sun and so has
everyone else in Laindon I expect!

**Barry**   Yer I did! And I've the right to call it shit-hole an'all
cos I had to fucking live there on the fucking tenth floor with
the fucking scum of the earth! Unlike Alan-fucking-Sugar
there!

*Silence.*

**Maureen**   Did you get moved in all right to your new place
Barry?

*Silence.*

**Barry**   There was bit of a delay cos the new flats weren't
connected to the electric for ages. But we're in now and
Jackie's made it all nice. You should come round. For a bit of
dinner.

*Silence.*

**Maureen**   I don't think your mother would be too happy.
Why don't you ask Shelley?

**Barry**   I'd love it if she come round.

**Maureen**   Well ask her.

**Barry** But will you come round? Mum's never bothered about me seeing you. Has she?

**Maureen** It's different Barry. You and Shelley have always kept out of it. And we've kept you out of it.

*Silence.*

**Maureen** D'you think it's unfair always coming to see us in Romford?

**Barry** It's neither here nor there.

*Silence.*

**Barry** Anyway we're hoping we're not going to be in the new place too long.

**Ken** Don't count your chickens Barry.

**Barry** We want our own place. Me and Jackie are sick of it. I know Shelley rents but she lives in London. Me and Jackie are the only one's in our family who are council. We want our own house. Where we can have a couple of kids.

**Maureen** How's it going?

**Ken** He's not got much lead in his pencil.

**Barry** I'm going to kill him in a minute.

*He gathers himself.*

**Barry** There's nothing wrong with the lead in my pencil. I've been thoroughly tested out. They're normal, there's plenty of them and they're first class swimmers.

**Ken** *kills himself laughing*.

**Barry** Ignore him, he's just a wind-up merchant.

**Ken** I told you, you should have come to work with me when you was sixteen. I said to Len, 'Your nephew Barry should come to work with me'. But you didn't want to do that.

*Silence.*

**Ken**   You'd have gone self-employed years ago. And you'd have your own house by now an'all. You can take a horse to water but you can't make him drink. And that's the truth.

**Barry**   Everyone makes mistakes Ken. I was on the waiting list for ten years for my own flat. So I could stand on my own two feet. And I've turned myself round haven't I? No, I didn't come and work for yer when I was sixteen. I was young. I was a tit.

**Ken**   Was?

**Barry**   Ha ha, very funny.

**Ken**   Boom, boom.

*Silence.*

**Barry**   Don't I deserve a second chance? Or is that it? Why shouldn't I have an house of my own? Why shouldn't I have a nice house to bring up a family? And be decent and normal. Everyone has got their own house except me.

**Maureen**   Your mum hasn't.

*Silence.*

**Barry**   You wished my mum dead Auntie Maureen.

*Silence.*

**Maureen**   There's many a time she's wished me dead and worse. I've had the letters off of her over the years.

**Barry**   That don't make it right.

**Maureen**   No, but it makes it equal.

*Silence.*

**Barry**   You're as bad as each other.

**Maureen**   I know we are darling.

**Barry**   You're like two schoolgirls.

**Maureen**   Perhaps we are.

**Barry**  You should be ashamed of yourselves.

**Maureen**  In a way darling I am.

**Barry**  Carrying on like it for years.

**Maureen**  Don't you think I've suffered?

**Barry**  And so has my mum.

**Maureen**  Barry.

**Barry**  It's pathetic.

**Maureen**  You've always stayed well out of it Barry and you should stay well out of it now.

**Barry**  All this fucking old time East End grudge-bearing and vendettas. We're not in Mare Street now Maur. We're in Basildon.

**Maureen**  Well if you haven't learned it by now Barry let me enlighten you. There's no new beginnings for families like ours. And there never has been. Things stay the same.

**Barry**  Well I'm not the same. And neither is your Shelley.

*Silence.*

I won't fall out with you Maureen. I've said me piece. But it's a crying shame you think like that.

*Silence.*

**Ken**  He didn't want this you know.

*Silence.*

He said if they start turn them out.

**Barry**  This is my mum's house.

**Maureen**  It might be your mother's home Barry but it's not her house.

*Silence.*

**Barry**  Here Ken, does your accountant know anything about VAT?

**Ken**    I should think so son, he's an accountant. Why?

**Barry**    Nothing.

*Silence.*

**Maureen**    Are you courting Ken? Or are you just having a bit of fun?

**Ken**    I am having a bit of fun. But, no I'm not courting at present.

**Maureen** *laughs and so does* **Ken**. **Doreen** *appears. Silence.*

*She goes to* **Len**.

**Doreen**    His breathing's changed. It's shallower. Haven't you been looking after him you rotten bastards?

*She tries to make* **Len** *more comfortable and on instinct* **Maureen** *helps.* **Doreen** *stops and lets* **Maureen** *take over.* **Barry** *and* **Ken** *stand uneasily. Silence.*

*Gradually everyone sits down and looks at* **Len**. *We can see his face a bit more clearly now. Silence.*

**Ken**    My old dad bought his plot twenty foot by hundred foot in 1934 when mum was carrying me. And he begged and borrowed. And no doubt he thieved an'all. To get that house of his up. And to think of it now. He brought all his materials by horse and cart from Stepney. All the way to Laindon. That's got to be a good twenty mile. My old man always said he was in the house with us the day Arthur Sweeney won the gold medal for the hundred yard sprint at the Empire Games. And the following day he was up in the Magistrates Court for not giving notice of building.

*He laughs.*

**Barry**    You are astonishing Ken.

**Ken**    What?

**Barry**    The shit that comes out of your mouth.

**Ken**    I'm trying to educate you.

**Barry**  Your old man built his own house?

**Ken**  Yer, he did son.

**Barry**  Well go on then.

**Ken** *smells something.*

**Ken**  Have you let one go?

**Barry**  No.

**Ken**  You want to go and sit on the toilet for half an hour.

**Barry**  It's probably him innit.

*They all look at* **Len**. **Ken** *shakes his head and tuts.*

**Ken**  That's shocking that is.

**Maureen**  Blaming it on your Uncle Len.

**Doreen**  Barry.

**Barry** *is shame-faced and hangs his head. Silence.*

*They all think.*

**Ken**  Yer, my old man built his own house in Basildon. And I was born in it. And I lived in it for twenty years until I was married. Authentic Basildon. I told yer. We was the Plotland People. There was thousands round all these areas. All the villages. Basildon, Laindon, Vange. People just trying to get out the slums in the East End. Loads a people came out here between the wars. Bought little plots of land and made a home. A new start.

*He laughs and looks at* **Len**. *Silence.*

*On a whim* **Ken** *whistles the tune to 'New York, New York'. It's too much for* **Doreen** *who stands and moves from her chair. She puts her head in her hands.* **Ken** *stops whistling. They all look at her. She composes herself. Silence.*

**Ken**  I've seen pictures of it round here. I can remember me mum and me dad talking. Some of them was like shacks, you know. And some of them was nice. Like bungalows. Apparently ours was rough and ready but me dad added to it. There wasn't no electric, no proper roads.

**Doreen** *sits back down and looks at* **Len**. *Silence.*

**Ken**    Obviously the Second World War come. And then after the war Labour came in and started building the new towns. And they saw what had already happened of its own course in the area.

*Silence.*

**Doreen** *looks at* **Maureen** *and then* **Barry**.

**Doreen**    Will you ask your Auntie Maureen if she heard that?

**Maureen**    Will you tell your mother, no I didn't.

*Silence.*

**Barry**    What is it mum?

**Doreen**    I think he's starting to rattle.

*They all listen.*

**Barry**    Shall I go and get the nurse?

**Maureen**    No.

*They all gather around* **Len**. *The reality of what is happening is beginning to hit home. Silence.*

**Barry**    Is he dying now mum?

**Doreen**    I think so babe.

*They all want to cry but don't. Silence.*

**Doreen**    Len, I love you. I love you darling.

*Silence.*

**Maureen**    I love you Lenny babe. I'm sorry Lenny.

*Silence.*

**Barry** *can hardly speak.*

**Barry**   I love you Uncle Len. You're the best dad I could ever have had.

*He takes all of his might not to cry. Silence.*

**Ken**   Good night and God bless old mate. I won't be too long and I'll come and find you.

*His shoulders move up and down as he attempts to hold himself together. Silence.*

**Len** *moves his head, as if yanked for a second into consciousness to gulp for his last breath, his eyes wide open and blazing for a moment before death. He dies. Silence.*

**Barry** *goes to his mum and they both cry.* **Maureen** *wipes her eyes alone. Silence.*

*The family gather and compose themselves.* **Maureen** *and* **Doreen** *look at each other. Very softly* **Ken** *begins to sing.*

**Ken**   'I'm forever blowing bubbles,
   Pretty bubbles in the air,
   They fly so high – .'

*He stops singing and looks at them all. Silence.*

He wanted us all to sing. He wanted us all to sing for him.

**Barry**   I can't do it Ken.

**Ken**   Yes you can son.

**Barry**   I can't.

**Ken**   Think how hard it is for me? I support Tottenham Hotspur.

*No one laughs. He encourages them to hold hands but* **Maureen** *and* **Doreen** *won't join hands.* **Ken** *ignores it.*

**Ken**   He wanted us to sing.

**Barry**   It's too much

**Ken**   When you nipped out did you ask the nurse Dor?

**Doreen** *nods. Silence.*

**Ken**   It's what he wanted. It's the sound he wanted to carry him into the night. Isn't it Doreen?

**Doreen** *nods.*

**Maureen**   I'll sing for him. I'll sing for my brother.

**Ken**   Will you sing Doreen if I start you off darling?

**Doreen** *nods. Then* **Barry** *nods.*

**Ken**   'I'm forever blowing bubbles –'

*They sing sweetly and full of love to carry him on his way.*

**Everyone**   '– Pretty bubbles in the air,
   They fly so high,
   Nearly reach the sky,
   Then like my dreams,
   They fade and die,
   Fortune's always hiding,
   I've looked everywhere,
   I'm forever blowing bubbles,
   Pretty bubbles in the air.'

*They finish and no one knows what to do.* **Doreen** *and* **Maureen** *look at* **Len**, *lifeless.* **Ken** *goes to* **Barry** *and holds him. They're all like that for a few moments.*

**Doreen**   Barry will you go and tell the nurse and she'll ring Dr Graham. Ken will you ring Pam next door. Just let it ring twice. She'll understand.

**Ken** *nods and then goes.* **Barry** *hesitates knowing the sisters will be left alone. He goes. Silence.*

**Doreen**   Will you help me lay him out?

**Maureen** *nods.*

**Doreen**   We're alone now Maur. Let's not.

**Maureen**   Its a long time since we've been alone together.

**Doreen** *nods. The sisters begin by pulling away the sheet, duvet and blanket from* **Len**'s *body.* **Maureen** *is slightly aghast as* **Doreen**

*removes* **Len**'s *urinary convene from his penis in a swift movement and puts it into a bowl by the bed. They arrange* **Len**'s *pyjamas and then lay out his body flat and straight. The sisters work well together folding the under sheet underneath* **Len**'s *arms and turning it over crisply.*

**Doreen** I'm glad I shaved him this morning now.

**Maureen** Did he know?

**Doreen** He hasn't spoken for a couple of days.

**Maureen** When did he last speak?

**Doreen** On Sunday morning.

**Maureen** What did he say?

**Doreen** *looks away as the sisters arrange the duvet and top blanket. Silence.*

**Doreen** *looks at* **Len** *and gently closes his eyes. She looks at* **Maureen**. *Silence.*

**Doreen** He asked for you.

**Maureen** Did he?

**Doreen** Yes.

**Maureen** *starts hitting herself with the open palm of her right hand across her forehead. She stills herself. Silence.*

**Maureen** You didn't tell me.

**Doreen** No.

**Maureen** I would have come.

**Doreen** You shouldn't have needed asking.

**Maureen** Why didn't you tell me?

**Doreen** Barry wanted you here. I didn't. Because I hate you. I hate your guts. I wish you nothing but the pain I feel inside. There.

**Maureen** *is stunned. Silence.*

**Maureen**    Hate?

**Doreen**    Yes that's right darling, hate.

*Silence.*

**Maureen**    There's going to be a reckoning before too long in this house darling.

**Doreen**    Yes there will darling.

**Maureen**    We're going to sort things out once and for all.

**Doreen**    You know Len's left the house to my Barry.

*Silence.*

**Doreen**    He hated him living on that estate. I'm sure there's something for you and Shelley. A keepsake.

**Maureen**    I don't believe you. He wouldn't do that. Not after everything that's happened.

**Doreen**    He made a will about five year ago. We both did.

*Silence.*

**Maureen**    Len wouldn't.

**Doreen**    You're not getting a tanner out of this house Maureen. And that's the end of it.

*Silence.*

**Maureen**    So you say.

**Doreen**    So I do say. Now don't you ever breathe a word in my direction again.

*Silence.*

*She kisses* **Len** *gently on his forehead. So does* **Maureen**. *The sisters look at each other. Silence.*

*Fade.*

## Act Two

*The same, a few days later.*

*Except the bed has been taken out of the room and the dining table is back in its rightful place.*

*And there are sympathy cards and some beautiful lilies.*

**Barry** *is eating a sandwich.*

*So is his wife,* **Jackie***, 35.* **Jackie***'s a big woman and she's in a Tesco uniform. They are also sharing some pickled onions from the jar.*

**Jackie**  You know you're gonna have to give me one tonight.

**Barry**  Babe, let me eat me sandwich in peace will you?

**Jackie**  I'm only saying.

**Barry**  I know.

**Jackie**  We didn't do it last night. I know you're upset about your Uncle Len but you've just got to get on with it.

**Barry**  I know.

**Jackie**  And if we don't do it tonight that's gonna be another month down the shit hole.

**Barry**  Fucking hell.

**Jackie**  Don't fucking hell me Barry, I'm ovulating.

*They eat. Silence.*

**Barry**  How much salad cream have you got on that sandwich?

**Jackie**  I dunno.

**Barry**  You heard what the gynaecologist said about your weight.

**Jackie**  And you fucking heard what he said about drinking and smoking. Prick.

**Barry**    You haven't said anything to Mum have you?

**Jackie**    No Barry that's your job.

**Barry**    She's going to go fucking spare.

**Jackie**    Well when we move in here and when we've got a family we can't have her here. I mean if we have IVF we could have twins. We could have triplets.

**Barry**    Don't give me nightmares.

**Jackie**    Well that's a nice thing to say.

**Barry**    Don't twist it.

**Jackie**    That's what you think is it?

**Barry**    No.

**Jackie**    You think having a baby's a nightmare!

**Barry**    Jackie darling, chill, chill. Take a chill pill.

**Jackie**    Don't you think I'm horny anymore?

**Barry** *puts his head in his hands.*

**Jackie**    I can stick me finger up your bum. Apparently its really good.

**Barry** *looks up. Silence.*

**Barry**    It's hard what with Uncle Len and all that. Course I fancy you.

**Jackie**    Shall we have a quick one now?

**Barry**    What?

**Jackie**    You always used to like a nosh on the train.

**Barry**    Jackie, they're upstairs.

**Jackie**    They'll be ages! You know I love a thrill in a bush!

**Barry**    No.

**Jackie**    Oh I'd love to do it while there's a vicar in the house!

**Barry**  Turn it in.

**Jackie**  Its right dirty.

**Barry**  Jackie.

**Jackie**  Go on let me ride yer.

**Barry**  Jackie, we've got Len lying in state in the front bedroom and the vicar and Mum in a prayer vigil. I know you've got the horn but there's a time and a place.

**Jackie**  Haven't you heard that sex and death are symbiotic to each other.

**Barry**  Do fucking what?

**Jackie**  You're thick as shit Barry, you really are.

*She laughs. Silence.*

**Jackie**  You're no fun anymore Barry.

*Silence.*

**Jackie**  There's a lot of men would love it on a plate like you get it. I never turn you down. Even when I'm on the blob.

**Barry** *shakes his head.*

**Jackie**  I'm always up for it. And at one time so were you. I don't know what's happened to you Barry.

*Silence.*

**Jackie**  And don't think I don't get offers. Men always fancy me. I could go out and get sex like that –

*She clicks her fingers.*

**Barry**  Well fucking go and get it then and see what happens.

*Silence.*

**Jackie**  I didn't mean it Barry.

**Barry**  I know you didn't.

**Jackie**  I'm stressed.

**Barry**   Don't be stressed. It doesn't help does it?

**Jackie**   You never tell me you love me no more Barry.

*Silence.*

**Jackie**   I can't wait until this house is ours. Baby'll be in the box room. It'll be Handy Manny this and Peppa Pig that, won't it Barry?

**Barry**   I hope so darling.

**Jackie**   There'll be school trips to the Wat Tyler Centre. And the little one can run around the Sonic Marshmallows.

**Barry**   What on earth is a Sonic Marshmallow?

**Jackie**   I don't know Barry but I know they've got 'em at the Wat Tyler Centre.

*Silence.*

**Barry**   Sometimes I think we've left everything too late.

**Jackie**   Don't worry Barry everything will be all right. I love you Barry.

**Barry** *nods. Silence.*

**Jackie**   What are them letters from the customs Barry? It's playing on me mind.

*Silence.*

**Barry**   Don't worry about it. Ken's accountant's on to it.

**Jackie**   Are you sure?

**Barry**   It's going to be a nightmare getting Mum in her own place.

**Jackie**   She can afford it. She's tight as arseholes. And she was only mouthing off to me the other day she's got fifty grand in savings and policies and what not.

**Barry**   I'll sort it.

**Jackie**   You better Barry because I ain't living here with her.

*They hear something. Silence.*

**Barry**  See. I told yer.

**Ken** *enters followed by* **Pam**.

**Ken**  Is he here then?

**Barry**  Who?

**Ken**  The vicar?

**Jackie**  Hello Ken.

**Ken**  Hello Jackie.

**Barry**  You been over the club?

**Ken**  No, got golf wrist ain't I?

**Jackie**  That's what they call it, is it?

**Ken**  It's what I call it.

**Jackie** *laughs. So does* **Ken**. *Silence*.

**Pam**  Doreen's asked me to do the catering. Have you got any requests?

*Silence.*

*She goes out. Silence.*

**Ken**  Strange woman, that Pam.

**Pam** *comes back in.*

**Pam**  You know Len dying's hit me hard. My Terry's got all emotionally possessive. Divorce has been mentioned. I said to Doreen, I said 'Dor, I can't go. I'm frightened of how I'm feeling. Anything could happen when I see poor Lenny –'

*She controls her emotions.*

'When I see him. In his little coffin to take him to heaven. I said I can't go Dor. I can't do it. Tell me what to do. Tell me what to do.' She said 'Pam get the kettle on and put out the spread'. And I thought that's what I'm going to do. I'm going to put out the best spread there's ever been. Wally's, ham sandwiches, jellied eels. Everything. Because that's what I can give. That's what I can contribute. I'd like to give more. I wish I could write a poem. I've tried. Sorry. I must go and powder my nose.

*She goes. Silence.*

**Barry**   Did Lenny ever give her one?

**Ken**   I think he must have.

*Silence.*

**Jackie**   Innit a shame Lenny never found no one.

**Barry**   He was one of life's bachelor types wasn't he?

*They hear noise. Silence.*

**Jackie**   I tell you what when we live here we're not having books in the toilet. It's weird.

**Barry**   Why can't you keep that fucking shut?

**Ken**   I told you Barry don't count your chickens.

**Jackie**   How's your accountant getting on with them letters from the VAT man Ken?

**Ken**   What letters?

**Barry**   Shut it, will yer, just fucking shut it! Jesus fucking Christ, when will you learn to keep that shut?

**Jackie** *is upset. There's noise.*

**Shelley**, *25, enters.*

*She is followed by her boyfriend,* **Tom**, *27. They're a pretty cool-looking couple.*

**Barry** *immediately stands.*

**Barry**   Hello Shell.

**Shelley**   Hello Barry, hello Jackie, I'm so sorry about Uncle Len. I'm so sorry we weren't here.

**Barry**  Don't you worry darling. Now who's this?

**Shelley**  Oh this is my fella Tom.

**Tom**  Hi. Hi.

*He shakes hands with everyone.*

**Jackie**  Hello darling, pleased to meet you.

**Ken**  Cor, look at you, haven't you grown up? You shouldn't be allowed to look like that. I remember singing to you on my knee.

**Barry**  Here Tom.

**Shelley**  Barry –

**Barry**  Here Tom. If you ever, ever do anything to hurt our Shell –

*Silence.*

**Shelley**  Barry –

**Barry**  If there's so much as a squeak out of our Shell you've looked at another tart, if you ever even think about laying so much as a finger on her, I'll come and find you, and I'll bite your nose off.

*Silence.*

And then when I'm done. He'll come looking for you.

*He points at* **Ken** *who very theatrically cracks his knuckles.*

**Tom** *looks at* **Shelley**. *He grins and the gulps and notices everyone looking at him.*

**Barry**  You've got to understand son, I love my cousin, but she's not like my cousin. We don't see so much of each other now but she's like my sister. We love each other don't we Shell? When Shelley was a nipper she used to say she wanted to marry me when she grew up.

**Shelley**  Shut up Barry.

**Barry**  It's the BFB. Come here son.

**Tom** *approaches* **Barry** *gingerly.* **Barry** *gives him a hug, kisses him on the cheek and rubs his hair.*

**Barry**   You're all right. Don't mind me. But you've got to have the hard word haven't you? You've got to have the hard word. It's nice to meet you son. I'm sorry I didn't catch you before.

**Tom**   I'm sorry I was away on a course.

**Jackie**   You and Shell will have to come round for a roast. Shelley's been promising for ages she'll come round. It's nice our new flat Shell.

**Barry**   Will yer come and see us Shell?

*Silence.*

**Shelley**   It's hard in term time. The weekends are really precious.

**Jackie**   Well it's not long till Christmas now is it?

**Shelley**   We're going to Tom's sister in Zurich.

**Jackie**   Well we're only up the 127, Shelley.

**Shelley**   Perhaps, you should come to ours?

**Jackie** *smarts and looks at* **Barry** *who keeps a low profile.*

**Shelley**   No? Okay.

**Ken**   Where's your mum?

**Shelley**   She's parking the car.

**Barry**   So how is Waltham-stan?

**Shelley**   Very funny.

**Barry**   Its like the black hole of Calcutta down there.

**Shelley**   You're such a racist dick Barry.

**Barry**   I call it like it is. Old school. Right Clarkson ain't I?

**Ken**   What you living in Walthamstow for?

**Shelley**  It's great.

**Ken**  It took us all donkeys years to get out of the East End and you've gone back in!

**Tom**  It's really good for transport links. And it's like Highgate in the village.

**Shelley**  We love it in the village. They've got a tapas bar and a deli. There are lots of like-minded people.

**Jackie**  Walthamstow's got a village?

**Barry**  I thought all Walthamstow had was the dog track?

**Tom**  Actually the greyhound stadium's closed.

**Jackie**  It's not.

**Tom**  They want to bulldoze it and turn it into flats. It's caused a bit of a fuss.

**Barry**  Didn't you know it had closed Jackie?

**Jackie**  I can't believe it. I had some nights in Charlie Chan's with my mate Sally.

**Ken**  I had a night out there with yer Uncle Len.

**Tom**  Charlie Chan's?

**Shelley**  Its some scuzzy old nightclub that used to be under the greyhound stadium.

**Jackie**  Have you ever been Shell?

**Shelley**  No.

**Jackie**  In my going out days it used to be red hot with the West Ham footballers. My best mate Sally had a slow dance up against the wall at Charlie Chan's with Frank McAvennie. I've always had my suspicions he's the father of her love child. My goddaughter, Francesca. Frank-Chesca. Know what I mean?

**Barry**  I do apologise Tom.

**Jackie**   Shut up you!

**Barry**   Is that reconditioned combi-boiler all right?

**Tom**   It's great thanks.

**Barry**   Now did Shelley tell you, I showed her how to bleed the radiators?

**Shelley**   It's fine Barry.

**Barry**   Cor. Your landlord paid up quick?

**Shelley**   They seem all right. We never have anything to do with them. I think they live in Suffolk or something. They've got money.

**Barry**   All right for some.

**Jackie**   Don't times change? Walthamstow dogs and Charlie's Chan's down the swanny. And the council demolishing the flats.

*She tuts and shakes her head.*

**Jackie**   Now you look like you've got some brains Tom. Do you know what a Sonic Marshmallow is when it's at home?

**Tom** *blushes and looks at everyone.*

**Tom**   Sorry, no.

**Jackie**   They've got them at the Wat Tyler Country Park apparently.

**Shelley**   I know what they are. I went there with my school on my probationary year.

**Jackie**   Well what are they then?

**Shelley**   They're large acoustic objects. You can hear each other whisper from fifty or sixty metres away.

**Barry**   You better stay away Jackie. You'll deafen half of Pitsea.

**Jackie**   And who's this Wat-his-name?

**Tom**  He started the Peasants' Revolt. It was a fourteenth-century attempt at a revolution.

**Shelley**  D'you know Fobbing?

**Barry**  Yer, I know it.

**Jackie**  Where is it?

**Ken**  It's near Thurrock.

**Barry**  I put new central heating in a cottage in Fobbing.

**Shelley**  It was one of the villages involved in the beginning of the Peasants' Revolt. It all started there and then Wat Tyler joined in from over the river in Kent.

**Jackie**  A revolution? In Essex?

**Tom** laughs. *No one else does. Silence.*

**Ken**  People always get the wrong idea about Essex don't they?

**Jackie**  Do they?

**Ken**  Well people always think about south Essex where London has spread out. Stacey Solomon and Romford Market. But there's old Essex. There's Colchester. That was the capital of Roman Britain, in its day. You've got Saffron Walden, that's pretty, for a ride out. Waltham Abbey, Thaxted. You've got your farmers. You've got your electronics industries around here and Chelmsford. Fords have still got a presence. You've got your construction industry. I mean you've got a lot of coastline there. Clacton, Frinton, Walton-on-the-Naze. They bring in your tourists a bit. Your travellers coming through Harwich. The idea all we are in Essex is a load of wide boys going and making a mint in the city's rubbish. Romford's not even in Essex anymore. London Borough of Havering innit?

**Jackie**  One of these days Barry's gonna take me up Walton-on-the-Naze.

**Barry** *looks at her.*

**Jackie**   What?

**Tom**   So what would you say defines Essex, Barry?

**Ken**   We've got spunk haven't we.

**Tom**   Spunk?

**Barry** *laughs.* **Ken** *laughs.*

**Ken**   What?

**Barry**   When they're that blatant I can't even be bothered to tee you up.

**Ken**   What?

**Barry**   You know.

**Ken**   It's the Blitz spirit out of the old East End. You can't get us down.

**Barry**   Pride in England innit, Shell?

**Shelley**   I've always thought there's something a bit Gypsy Lee about Essex. Its the hard, bright eyes. Scousers are the same.

**Jackie**   There's nothing pikey about Essex, Shell, and as for saying we're the same as Scousers? That's bang out of order.

**Tom**   So what happened when an old Anglo-Saxon county was faced with mass migration out of the East End of London?

**Barry**   Magic, Tom, pure magic. That's what happened. People with get up and go.

**Ken**   He was a late developer.

**Barry**   Boom, boom.

*He laughs and shakes his head.*

**Shelley**   Wanting something better and old English conservatism equals right-wing materialism in my experience Tom.

**Jackie**  I can't understand a word you're saying Shelley but I know it ain't nice.

*Silence.*

**Tom**  Well this is fascinating. Really. I've been thinking about this sort of debate loads. For my play. Really. Fascinating discussion.

**Barry**  What's that?

**Tom** *blushes and feels very shy. Silence.*

**Ken**  Don't you two want to buy yer own place?

**Tom**  We can't afford it.

**Shelley**  It's a bit early doors for that. We've only just moved in together. And we haven't got a deposit anyway Ken. And we couldn't get a mortgage. London's expensive.

**Ken**  Why don't you come out here? You can get a job in a school in Basildon.

**Shelley**  We don't really want to live in Basvegas, thanks. It's not us. And Tom's a writer. What's he going to do in Basildon? Anyway, we don't know what all the fuss is about buying your own house. You pay thousands of pounds in interest. And if you go to Europe you they have a completely different attitude to property. Much healthier. Making a home not owning a house.

**Jackie**  There's nothing wrong with Basildon, Shelley.

*Silence.*

**Ken**  Are you a writer son?

**Barry**  You never told me he was a writer Shell? I thought he was a teacher an'all?

**Shelley**  Well Tom's written a script and its really good and he's been offered a place on the BBC Writers Academy. They train the writers up and they write *Doctors*, and if it all goes well. Which it will because Tom's a brilliant writer then he gets to write an episode of *Holby City*.

**Ken**   Fantastic. Well done son.

**Ken** *squeezes* **Tom***'s cheek, which hurts a bit.*

**Tom**   I'm not really a writer. I'm a teacher. I teach English.

*He becomes incredibly shy. Silence.*

**Jackie**   *Holby City*? Really? Are you famous? Is he famous? Are you famous?

**Barry**   Jackie hc's talking darling! So what plays have you done?

**Tom**   I took a show to Edinburgh with my Theatre Studies group and it was a hit. I wrote it. And people have taken an interest.

*He blushes with a mixture of pride and shyness.*

**Ken**   I have trod on the boards in my time. I was a leading light in the Vange Players. I was the one who dies in *Abigail's Party*.

**Barry**   I've heard it all now.

**Ken**   I was.

**Barry**   More like the Vagina Players.

**Ken**   Now tell me Tom, is that your name again?

**Tom**   Yes.

**Ken**   Have you been to see *The Jersey Boys*?

**Tom**   No.

**Ken**   Well treat yourself and Shelley to a couple of tickets and go. Its bloody marvellous.

**Jackie**   Oh, have you been to see *Mamma Mia!*?

**Tom**   No, we've not caught it, yet. Have we?

**Shelley**   No.

**Ken**   Well I tell you what son, if you can write one of them musicals you can kiss Walthamstow goodbye.

**Barry**   What does your old man do then Tom?

**Shelley**   Barry, you're giving him the third degree.

**Tom**   He's an investment banker.

**Barry**   Nice. Can't you tap him up for a deposit?

**Shelley**   Tom and his dad don't speak.

**Tom**   The less said about my father the better. What do you do?

**Ken**   I'm retired son. I had a successful business going. Plumbing, central heating and all that jazz. I had ten men working for me. You know it was the eighties.

**Barry**   Turn it in.

**Ken**   You have ups and downs. But people always need their heating and their hot water. We was always busy.

**Barry**   Until Blair and his mob let the doors open to half of Europe.

**Ken**   I taught young Barry there everything he knows. And he didn't fucking know one end of a spanner from another. Did you?

**Barry**   You'd think he was Theo Paphitis the way he fucking talks.

**Jackie**   Language Barry.

**Tom**   And are you married Ken? Have you got any children?

**Ken**   Sadly my wife passed away.

**Tom**   I'm sorry.

**Ken**   Long time ago now. I've got four kids. They're all like me. Outward bound.

**Doreen** *and* **Reverend David Williams** *enter.*

*He's about 50. He looks at his wristwatch.*

**Reverend David Williams**    Hello, hello. Well we should have a talk about what I'm going to say about Leonard.

**Barry** *and* **Jackie** *stand up and make way for* **Doreen** *and* **Reverend David Williams** *to sit at the dining table.*

**Barry**    It's Lenny.

**Ken**    That's right. Or Len.

**Shelley**    Hello Auntie Doreen, I'm sorry about Uncle Len.

*She approaches* **Doreen** *and she lets her niece kiss her on the cheek. Silence.*

**Doreen** *turns away from* **Shelley** *without saying a word or looking at her.* **Shelley** *looks at everyone.* **Barry** *shakes his head.*

**Shelley**    This is my boyfriend Tom.

**Doreen** *looks at him and nods.* **Tom** *hesitates, unsure whether to approach.*

**Tom**    Hello, I'm very sorry about Lenny.

**Doreen**    So I am doll, so am I.

*There's noise and then* **Maureen** *enters. She goes to the dining table and sits right down. On reflex* **Reverend David Williams** *stands.*

**Maureen**    Don't mind me. I'm only the other sister.

**Reverend David Williams** *looks at* **Doreen** *who nods. He sits down.*

**Barry**    Would you like a Bell's, Reverend? Drop of Scotch?

*He looks at* **Maureen** *and then* **Doreen**.

**Reverend David Williams**    Yes please.

*Barry goes in search of one in the drinks cabinet.*

**Reverend David Williams**    Well if everyone's here. We should talk about the service and what you would like me to say.

*He takes a pad and a pen from his pocket.*

**Reverend David Williams**    Hymns?

**Jackie**    Can we have 'Lord of the Dance'?

**Doreen**    Jackie darling, it's not a karaoke.

**Jackie**    Can't we have something that's not depressing?

**Ken**    He wanted 'Abide with Me'.

**Doreen**    Did he?

**Ken**    He loved it. Cup Final Day. The massed bands. 'Abide with Me'. Len always had a tear in his eye at kick-off on Cup Final Day.

**Maureen**    That's a lovely idea Ken.

**Reverend David Williams**    Any objection?

**Doreen** *shakes her head.* **Barry** *appears with the bottle of Scotch and a glass.*

**Reverend David Williams**    Might I suggest Psalm 23. Sung. 'The Lord Is My Shepherd'.

*He takes the glass and* **Barry** *pours him a very large Scotch. The* **Reverend** *takes a large gulp.*

**Barry**    Down the hatch father!

*He laughs. Silence.*

**Doreen**    Yes that's fine. Will you ask her if it's fine?

**Reverend David Williams** *takes another large gulp.* **Barry** *decides to leave the vicar the bottle.*

**Maureen**    You can tell her it's fine by me.

**Barry**    I'm sorry Shelley.

**Shelley**    I'm sorry for you Barry.

*Silence.*

**Ken**    Could I, er. Erm, Reverend, as erm Len's friend.

**Reverend David Williams**    Let's hear from the family first and then we'll come to friends. All in good time.

*He attends to his pad and pen.*

So, Leonard.

**Ken**   Len or Lenny.

**Reverend David Williams**   Len, was born when?

**Maureen**   1950. March.

**Doreen**   We was out of the East End.

**Maureen**   Three rooms in Mare Street. Mum and Dad had two and then they had three.

**Doreen**   We come out to Romford in 1970 first of all.

**Reverend David Williams**   Romford first?

**Doreen**   Loads of them did didn't they? Loads of them. Out of the East End. To Romford, Billericay, Basildon, Chelmsford. All moved out there. Looking for something better.

**Maureen**   Mum and Dad got an old GLC mortgage.

**Reverend David Williams**   And Len came with you?

**Doreen**   Well he was always inclined to be a bit of a mummy's boy was Len. He wasn't a poof or nothing.

**Maureen**   He was a bit of ladies man as it goes.

**Ken**   He liked a bit of skirt.

**Reverend David Williams** *laughs a bit too loudly. Everyone is uneasy.*

**Doreen**   He packed in his job at the garage on Kenton Road and he come with us.

**Reverend David Williams**   What did he do?

**Maureen**   Well he was a mechanic. He was apprenticed as a mechanic.

**Reverend David Williams**   Right.

**Doreen**   But he said to Mum and Dad he wanted to come to Romford with everyone

**Maureen**   He said he was going to get a job at Fords.

**Doreen**   And he did an'all. Fords at Dagenham. He got our dad a job there as well.

**Maureen**   He always drove a Ford did Len. Cor. He loved his first Granada. And he worked for Fords all his life.

**Doreen**   He was quite senior in the end. Before he got ill. You know management. He worked in Brentwood. Don't ask me what he did. I don't understand it. He wore a shirt and tie most days.

**Reverend David Williams**   So how did he end up in Basildon? In this house.

**Doreen**   That's another story.

**Maureen**   Go on, Dor. We'd all like to hear it.

*Silence.*

**Jackie**   I can't handle this.

**Maureen**   Then go and put the kettle on darling. If you can prize it from the grip of Pam next door.

**Jackie**   Barry why don't you say something? This ain't right.

**Barry** *motions a gesture to* **Jackie** *for her to keep quiet. She shakes her head and leaves.*

**Shelley**   Tom, why don't you go for a walk round the block?

**Tom**   What?

**Shelley**   Go for a walk round the block. Now.

**Tom** *exits. Silence.*

**Reverend David Williams** *pours himself another Scotch and has a gulp.*

**Reverend David Williams**   And did Len travel?

**Maureen**   No, he didn't travel.

**Doreen**   He was frightened of flying.

**Maureen**   He wanted to.

*Silence.*

**Reverend David Williams**   Did he have any hobbies?

**Ken**   You can sum it up in three words.

**Barry**   West Ham United.

**Ken**   He loved the Chicken Run in the old days but he's had a season ticket in the Bobby Moore for the last eight years. Sir Trevor Brooking's our Len's all-time hero. I mean he had a soft spot for Bobby Moore course and Paulo Di Canio. But Sir Trevor was the one Lenny worshipped.

**Reverend David Williams**   Well I'll make sure I mention football.

**Ken**   We've got to have 'Bubbles' in the crematorium.

**Barry**   The 1975 Cup Final version. It's got to be the 1975 Cup Final version.

**Ken**   And he wants a bubble machine in the church.

**Barry**   Does he?

**Ken**   Will that be all right Reverend?

**Reverend David Williams**   I'll have to have a talk to the Diocese.

**Ken**   What about?

**Reverend David Williams**   Health and safety.

**Ken**   For a bubble machine?

**Barry**   This is going from the sublime to the ridiculous here.

**Ken**   Take it from me Reverend, as a former captain of industry, a bubble machine is not a fire hazard.

**Barry** *laughs. Silence.*

**Doreen**   You seem to know an awful lot about what our Len wanted and what he didn't want Ken?

**Maureen**   This ain't the time for laughing and joking Ken.

**Ken**   Well seeing as you ask –

**Reverend David Williams** *is a touch tipsy now.*

**Reverend David Williams**   Any important beliefs? Feelings about the world? Life? Important friendships?

**Doreen**   Ask Ken about that.

**Maureen**   They was mates from the time we first moved here.

**Ken**   Look here, before we go any further –

**Barry**   He liked a round of golf. You can put that down.

**Ken**   I need to straighten this out.

**Barry**   He liked a bit of a sing and a dance. He could do an half decent Nat King Cole.

**Doreen**   He liked a book. There's even books in our toilet. He was educated. He educated himself did Len.

**Shelley**   Uncle Len always did a lot for charity. He was in the Basildon Rotary Club. And he always organized Children in Need at Fords. He'd be out and about in Basildon shaking a bucket. Wasn't he?

**Barry**   Had me at it as well.

**Doreen**   He always helped the worse off.

**Maureen**   He certainly did.

**Ken** *coughs loudly. Silence.*

**Barry**   What's up Ken? Need a Fisherman's Friend?

**Ken**   Touché Barry.

**Doreen**   He was like a lot of people round here. He worked hard. He never asked no one for nothing. You know he left school when he was fourteen and he was never out of work in forty-five years. He adored Margaret Thatcher. He was into politics and watching the news, was Len. He had to watch *Newsnight* with his hot chocolate before he went to bed. He said it was the worst thing this country ever did when they turfed Maggie out.

**Reverend David Williams**   I can't say I agree with him there!

*He laughs a bit too hard again. Everyone is uneasy, again.*

**Doreen**   He wasn't workshy our Len.

**Maureen**   Shame he had you leeching off of him.

**Shelley**   Mum.

**Doreen**   He worshipped his family.

**Maureen**   Well some of them anyway.

**Doreen**   Don't start darling.

**Maureen**   Don't you start darling.

**Barry**   Mum. Maur. We are in the presence of a representative on earth of God. Okay?

*He points to the ceiling.*

Uncle Len's up there. And I tell you what, after we've said goodbye to him, you can scratch each other's eyes out for all I care. I've done with it. But until then I don't want another pissy remark out of either of you. Understood?

**Shelley**   Are you listening Mum?

**Doreen**   Don't play the hard man Barry. It doesn't suit you darling.

**Barry**   Don't you dare. Things will be said.

**Doreen**   Will they?

**Shelley**   That's right. Mum.

**Maureen**   I'm not deaf darling.

**Barry**   I do apologise. For my language, Reverend, Father. But there's a lot of. Difficulties. In a manner of speaking.

**Reverend David Williams**    Yes. Yes. There is.

*Silence.*

I think we should pray for friendship and love. Let's pray together.

*He looks at them all and one by one they lower their heads. He closes his eyes and clasps his hands in prayer. Silence.*

*They all look at each other. Then* **Maureen** *closes her eyes and clasps her hands and all the others follow – except* **Shelley** *who rolls her eyes and folds her arms.*

**Reverend David Williams**    Lord, behold the family here assembled. We thank you for the place in which they dwell. For the love that unites them. For the peace accorded to us this day. For the hope with which we expect the morrow.

**Ken** *starts to get the giggles and so does* **Shelley**. *Even* **Maureen** *and* **Doreen** *look like they might start to laugh.* **Barry** *remains resolute and scowls at the others. The* **Reverend** *pauses and draws breath and then continues, speaking up. The family feel ashamed.*

**Reverend David Williams**    For the health, the work, the food and the bright skies. That make our lives delightful. For our family. And for our friends. In all the parts of the earth. Amen.

**Everyone**    Amen.

**Barry**    Thank you.

*They all open their eyes and unclasp their palms relieved.*

**Reverend David Williams**    Almighty Father, eternal God, hear our prayers for Len.

*They all close their eyes and pray again – except* **Shelley** *who decides to wander out of the room.*

**Reverend David Williams**    Lord Jesus, our Redeemer, You willingly gave Yourself up to death so that all people might be saved and pass from death into a new life. Hear our prayers. Look with love on Your people who mourn and pray for their dead brother. Lord Jesus, You alone are holy and compassionate. Forgive our brother Len his sins. By dying You opened the gates of life for those who believe in You. Do not let Len be parted from You. But by Your glorious power give him light, joy, and peace in heaven where You live. For ever and ever. Amen.

**Everyone**   Amen.

*They open their eyes and unclasp their hands.* **Barry** *and* **Maureen** *notice* **Shelley** *has slipped out.*

**Doreen**   Thank you.

**Maureen**   Yes, thank you.

**Doreen**   I'm only sorry I don't come to the church more often.

**Reverend David Williams**   Well I think I have everything I need for the eulogy. I'm sorry there is unhappiness and discord in this house.

*Silence.*

Saint Paul wrote to Timothy.

**Barry**   Who?

**Reverend David Williams**   'We brought nothing into the world; for that matter we cannot take anything with us when we leave, but if we have food and covering we may rest content.'

*Silence.*

**Reverend David Williams**   Thank you, thank you for the. Hospitality. I'll see you next week.

**Tom** *appears.*

**Tom**   Where's Shelley?

**Maureen**   I don't know Tom.

**Ken**  He didn't want the vicar giving the eulogy. He wasn't religious. Len wanted someone who knew him.

**Reverend David Williams**  I see. Well.

**Barry**  Ken, turn it in.

**Doreen**  And who else is going to do it?

**Maureen**  I'm not doing it. And if I'm not doing it, she's not doing it.

**Ken**  He wanted me to do it. He wanted jokes. Funny stories.

*Silence.*

**Barry**  If that's what he wanted why didn't you say earlier?

**Ken**  I've been trying to get a word in edgeways for half an hour here.

**Doreen**  You know Ken it's beginning to get on my wick. Len wanted this, Len wanted that.

**Ken**  I'm sorry Dor.

**Doreen**  Spit it out Ken.

**Ken**  It's the way he wanted it.

**Doreen**  Wanted what?

**Ken**  He didn't want you to know what he wanted for the end until the end. Because he didn't want the arguing. He was sick to his high teeth with it.

*Silence.*

**Doreen**  So you said.

**Ken**  He didn't want you knowing what he wanted for the funeral until it was being planned because he knew what you and Maureen would be like.

*Silence.*

**Doreen**  Well? What did he want?

**Ken**   He wanted a lot of things. It's all here. Exactly, how he wanted the funeral. The wake.

*He takes a piece of paper from his pocket which he gives to* **Doreen**. *She looks at it.*

**Maureen**   All these surprises are making me wonder what else you've got up your sleeve?

**Doreen**   It says here: 'Ken to read letter about the contents of my will.'

*Silence.*

**Ken**   Yer, that's right.

**Barry**   You what?

*Silence.*

**Ken**   He changed his will.

**Barry**   He what?

**Doreen**   He couldn't have.

**Ken**   He did. He did it two month ago. I had to take him to see his solicitor. I had to sit outside in the reception with the wheelchair while they did their business.

**Maureen** *breaks out into a big smile.* **Barry** *and* **Doreen** *look at each other.*

**Maureen**   God bless you Lenny. God bless you.

**Barry**   What's he done?

**Ken**   I don't know Barry. I don't know what he's done. But I told you. I told yer. Don't count your chickens.

*Silence.*

**Doreen**   I see.

**Maureen**   God bless you Len. I knew it.

**Ken**   I've got to collect a letter from the solicitor the morning of the funeral. At nine o'clock on the dot. Len wants me to read it out at the wake.

**Doreen** *turns away from* **Ken**. *Silence.*

**Reverend David Williams** *stands uneasily.*

**Reverend David Williams**    Well there's nothing more for me to do here.

*He sways on the way out. He stops dead still to compose himself.*

**Barry**    Are you all right?

**Reverend David Williams**    You'll let me know this afternoon if you want me to speak the eulogy?

**Barry** *nods.*

**Ken**    Goodbye Father. Be lucky.

**Reverend David Williams** *sways as he goes.* **Barry**, **Doreen** *and* **Maureen** *look at* **Ken**. **Tom** *goes. Silence.*

**Ken**    Well there's no use losing any sleep over it. There's a week Monday until the funeral.

*He goes.* **Barry** *hangs his head. Silence.*

**Doreen**    Well we'll have to see, won't we doll?

**Maureen**    Yes doll, we will.

*The sisters look at each other. Silence.*

*Fade.*

*Interval.*

## Act Three

*The same, a week and two days later.*

*Except the dining table has been pushed against one wall, and the sofa against another wall so there is space in the room for the wake.*

*Another little mismatching table has been found and is beside the larger dining table. Covering both tables is food and drink and plastic cutlery and paper plates. Everything you'd expect to see there at an old school East End or Essex wake, with two tubs of jellied eels taking up a good amount of the space in the middle, is there.*

**Tom** *and* **Pam** *sit side by side on two dining table chairs in the middle of the room. They're drinking wine.*

**Tom**  I'm writing something new. Something that relates to ordinary working people. Why shouldn't they have theatre for them? Why shouldn't ordinary working people have a half-decent theatre for them?

**Pam**  Like what?

**Tom**  I don't know. Something brilliant and fantastical. The interactivity of the reality show and the thrill of the game show. The high-mindedness of Ibsen and Chekhov and a sentimental song and a silly joke. One big, rich, fabulous meal.

**Pam**  Sounds like a bit of dog's dinner to me.

**Tom**  Why should you, or Shelley's family be limited to the crap that's on the television or whatever Hollywood rubbish they've got on at the multiplex. Or whatever guff tours into the Towngate? That's the local theatre isn't it? Or have to pay through the nose to see a musical in the West End? Where are the plays and shows about you? And for you? It makes me angry. I want to tell new stories. In new ways. I once went to the National Theatre. I looked at it and I thought I can't set foot in that place. I thought it's not a national theatre, it's a middle-class theatre. And the liberal middle class, at that. I walked away. And broke into a run.

*He smiles to himself, feeling clever.*

Like Maupassant from the Eiffel Tower. Horrified. Not just at the ugliness of the building. It made my head hurt. The thought of all those middle-class people playing dress-up.

**Pam**  I thought your dad was a banker? So Doreen said.

**Tom**  I'm so embarrassed I went to a private school I can't tell you. But I'm working class in here. Inside. I'm with you Pam.

*He puts his hand across his chest. He looks at her. She laughs.*

**Pam**  You are cute. Those hands don't look like they've done a hard day's work in their life. Are you little bit tipsy Tom?

*He smiles.*

**Tom**  Ordinary working people deserve something more. If you look at the history at one time the theatre gave a voice to the white working class. To the man in the street. I often think now, the theatre's embarrassed of him.

**Pam**  Never mind about the theatre mate. I work for the council and these cuts are gonna bite after Christmas.

*He nods.*

**Tom**  I like Shakespeare. Have you ever seen a Shakespeare play?

**Pam**  No darling. Wouldn't like to.

**Tom**  He was for everyone. I often think answers lie in the past. God, I feel so awful. I've got this place on the Writers Academy. But I don't want it. I want to make art. But, being a playwright, which is what I really want to be, doesn't pay any money. So I need to go on the course at the BBC and try and find a way of earning some money. It's not really what I want to do. But I want to have a future with Shelley. I really like her.

**Pam**  You're young, don't you worry about that.

*Silence.*

**Tom**   I'm sorry, I'm going on. I'm being an idiot. You don't want to hear about this. I think I am a bit drunk.

**Pam**   You shouldn't have a go at the Towngate.

**Tom**   I know, I'm sorry, I've never been. This is only the second time I've been to Basildon.

**Pam**   They put on some right good things people enjoy. Me and Doreen have booked up to see Des O'Connor.

*Silence.*

And I like the telly. I love all my programmes. *Corrie, Strictly Come Dancing. I'm a Celebrity Get Me Out of Here.* It's just a bit of fun. Innit?

**Tom**   We don't watch them.

**Pam**   I work with old people and when you've done a day's work. Literally wiping the arses of the infirm and senile I want to put me feet up and chill out. I don't want people trying to explode me brain with all the shit in the world and telling me what's good for me. Not when I've done a hard day's work. I tell my Terry, turn the news off, it's depressing.

*He nods. She thinks.*

**Pam**   If I read you my poem will you tell me what you think?

**Tom**   Okay.

*She takes out a piece of paper from her pocket and reads it aloud.*

**Pam**   'Len, Len, Len: I'll never forget: That afternoon; Way back when.'

*Silence.*

*She wipes a tear away and puts the paper back in her pocket.*

**Pam**   What do you think?

**Tom**   It's lovely.

**Pam**  You're a good fella. Shelley's lucky.

*He drinks.*

**Tom**  So did you and Len?

**Pam**  I admit he has, from time to time, stirred the porridge. But it wasn't that. It was him. He was lovely.

*Silence.*

**Pam**  Doreen said you don't speak to your dad?

**Tom**  We disagree about almost everything there is to disagree on. He didn't want me to train as a teacher after university. He wanted me to follow him into banking. So we fell out. I hate my father and everything he stands for. It's his sort of money-grabbing capitalism that's destroying the world.

**Pam**  Well it's good to know its not just people like us who have fall outs.

**Tom**  No.

*He drinks, so does she.*

**Pam**  How come you didn't go to the funeral?

**Tom**  Shelley was afraid there'd be a scene.

*He thinks.*

**Tom**  Do you think Len's left you anything in his will?

**Pam**  Why does Shelley think he has?

*There's noise.* **Ken** *enters followed by* **Maureen** *and* **Shelley**. **Ken** *heads straight to the buffet and peels back some cellophane.*

**Pam**  Mittens off Ken.

**Ken** *withdraws his hand.*

**Shelley**  I need a cuddle.

*She heads out and* **Tom** *follows her. The others watch them go.*

**Shelley**  Come and get me before you read Uncle Len's letter.

**Ken** *nods. They exit.*

**Pam**    Tea? Coffee? It's bitter out there.

**Maureen**    Tea please Pam.

**Ken**    I'll have a cuppa. Strong. Two sugars.

**Pam** *goes out.*

**Maureen**    I appreciate the lift, Ken.

**Ken**    No problem Maur.

**Maureen**    I appreciate it all the same.

*Silence.*

**Ken**    You all right?

**Maureen**    Yer.

*Silence.*

**Ken**    When was the last time you had a fella?

**Maureen**    Not for a while.

**Ken**    No?

**Maureen**    I tried that internet dating but it didn't work for me.

**Ken**    I take it you'll accept a Facebook friend request?

*She laughs and looks at him.*

**Ken**    I tell you what you've certainly got the edge on Doreen as you've got older.

*She walks and looks at the spread.*

**Ken**    It's a shame you and your sister can't patch it up.

**Maureen**    Never.

**Ken**    You're both divorced and on your own. You've both got your kids off of your hands. You work in Asda in Romford. Doreen works in Tesco's in Laindon. You could be the best of friends.

**Maureen**   No Ken. There's no chance of that.

**Ken**   Why?

*Silence.*

**Maureen**   You can take me out if you like? I haven't been fucked in a long time.

**Pam** *enters with two cups of tea.*

**Pam**   I know you like a Bournville, Ken, but there's none in the cupboard so you'll have to make do with a chocolate finger.

**Ken** *and* **Maureen** *take their tea and* **Pam** *goes out.*

**Maureen**   I know you like me.

**Ken**   Yer, I do.

**Maureen**   You a handsome man Ken.

**Ken**   I know.

*She laughs. So does he. At that precise moment* **Doreen** *enters. Silence.*

**Doreen**   Don't mind me.

**Ken**   Dor.

**Doreen**   You can tell her, that I've already tried to get you to open Len's letter today, so a lot of good her slagging around will do her.

**Ken**   I don't know what you're on about Dor.

**Maureen**   It's not about that darling.

*She goes out.* **Doreen** *watches her go and then looks at* **Ken***.*

**Ken**   She wasn't after knowing about the will Dor.

**Doreen**   What was she after then?

**Ken**   I don't know Dor.

**Doreen**   I know.

**Ken**   Well you tell me?

**Doreen**   Don't mug me off Ken.

**Ken**   I'm not Dor.

**Doreen**   Don't.

**Ken**   I'm not.

**Doreen**   Don't do it.

**Ken**   I'm not doing anything.

**Doreen**   She's after your money Ken.

**Ken**   What?

**Doreen**   She's after your money.

*Silence.*

**Ken**   And what are you after Dor?

**Doreen**   I don't know what you mean Ken?

**Ken**   I heard you.

**Doreen**   What?

**Ken**   Len was on his death bed.

**Doreen**   What?

**Ken**   'It's a long time since I've known the feeling of a strong man'?

**Doreen**   It's true.

**Ken**   You could have knocked me down with a feather.

**Doreen**   Don't you like me no more Ken?

**Ken**   You had your chance with me a long time ago.

**Doreen**   I know and I was silly.

*He gets caught. He gulps back the emotion.*

**Ken**   This is too much today. Once I got over the shock of being on my own I would have taken you on in a shot. And married you. Len could have lived his life.

*Silence.*

**Ken**  And I was still good to you and your Barry and he was nothing more than a yob.

**Doreen**  I know.

**Ken**  And all you ever did was turn your nose up at me.

*Silence.*

**Doreen**  I didn't.

*Silence.*

**Ken**  You're only interested in sticking your head above the parapet now because your sister's shown an interest in me. I'm too old to play games Doreen.

**Doreen**  I'm not playing games Ken.

**Ken**  I know I don't look it but I'm seventy-five years of age.

*Silence.*

**Doreen**  It never seemed right going with you. You was Lenny's best mate.

*Silence.*

**Ken**  Don't take me for a fool Doreen. I've haven't got a clue what Lenny's put in this letter.

**Doreen**  I know.

**Ken**  But you must know Dor, if Lenny's left this house to Barry. And that part of the will's not been altered, Barry and Jackie won't have you here living with them.

**Doreen**  You don't know nothing. My Barry wouldn't do that. And as for Jackie, she wouldn't have a job in Tesco's if it wasn't for me.

**Ken**  You must think I'm a right one.

**Doreen**  I don't.

**Ken**   Very convenient. Just when you're out of house and home. You think you can wrap your legs around me and in a flash and a bang you've got me where you want me. And if you're lucky you might get a few quid out of me when I'm gone. Like some silly old sod. And I'll have you shacked up with me in five minutes telling me what I can do and what I can't do.

**Doreen**   No. I've always liked you Ken. But when you've been shit on once by a man and you're bringing up a child.

*Silence.*

And all this about Barry and Jackie I've never heard such a load of crap in all my life. This is my home. I don't care whose name's on the deeds I've been here for thirty years. And I'm not going anywhere.

**Ken**   Open your eyes Doreen. Open your eyes.

**Doreen**   All Maureen wants you for is your money.

**Ken**   And what do you want me for? You sponged off your brother for most of your years and now he's gone you want another lemon.

*Silence.*

**Doreen**   No, it's love. It's love.

**Ken**   Love?

**Doreen**   I've loved you for years. You make me laugh. I love it when you put your hand on my shoulder, or round me, or on my hand without even thinking twice. It keeps me awake at night. The life I could have had. With you.

*Silence.*

**Ken**   Well it's too late.

**Doreen**   It's not.

*Silence.*

**Ken**   I'm sorry Dor but I don't believe you darling.

*He goes. She is devastated. She pulls herself together. Silence.*

**Barry** *and* **Jackie** *enter.* **Barry** *is wearing a black suit and black tie round his neck but instead of a white shirt with collar he's sporting a West Ham United away jersey under his suit. Silence.*

**Barry** *and* **Doreen** *look at each other.*

**Barry** Mum?

**Doreen** So I'm going to be out on my ear am I?

**Barry** Mum.

**Doreen** *shakes her head and goes out.* **Barry** *looks at* **Jackie***.*

**Barry** What have you said?

**Jackie** I haven't said nothing!

*He shakes his head and takes out his iPhone and looks at it.*

**Jackie** You will ask Ken for help with his accountant won't you Barry? Before he goes.

*He shakes his head at the content on his iPhone.*

**Barry** Avram Grant? More like Avram Can't.

**Shelley** *comes in followed by* **Tom***. They hesitate and look at* **Barry** *and* **Jackie***.* **Tom** *goes to the table and pours himself some more wine.*

**Barry** Here gets us a Foster's Tom.

**Tom** *passes* **Barry** *a can of Foster's.*

**Shelley** You all right Barry?

**Barry** Not really.

**Shelley** I'm sorry.

**Barry** Shell.

**Shelley** Yeah?

**Barry** Whatever's in this letter of Uncle Len's –

**Shelley** Yeah?

**Barry**   We've always stayed out of the shit between my mum and your mum haven't we?

**Shelley**   Course Barry.

**Barry**   Whatever Uncle Len's done he's done.

**Shelley**   Yeah, of course.

**Barry**   And he must have his reasons.

**Shelley**   Yeah.

**Barry**   You know I love you Shell.

**Shelley**   I love you Barry. You're not my cousin. You're my big bro. The BFB.

**Barry**   I think the world of you darling.

**Shelley**   Barry.

**Barry**   So there's not going to be any aggro between us is there?

**Shelley**   No Barry. Never.

*Silence.*

**Jackie**   I would have thought you'd put your own wife first. And as for you doll. You might have your cousin wrapped around your little finger but you're no better than me darling.

*She goes out.* **Barry** *follows. Silence.*

**Shelley**   Don't drink any more.

**Tom**   Okay.

**Shelley**   This is all so vulgar. I hate it. I hate Basildon. I hate Essex.

**Tom**   It's part of you.

**Shelley**   Yep, it's the part of me I hate.

**Tom**   They're your people. You can't dismiss them just because you don't agree with them.

**Shelley**   I can. I don't like them.

**Tom**   What? Because you don't share their values? People like your family deserve to be heard. And if we don't agree then all the more reason.

**Shelley**   They are heard Tom. Pick up a copy of the *Sun* or the *Daily Mail*. And you'll hear it barking at you loud and clear.

**Tom**   That's not them. That's the Rothermeres and the Murdochs of the world.

**Shelley**   It's all right for you, you're not related to them.

**Tom**   Empathy Shelley.

**Shelley**   Why don't you empathise with your dad?

*He drinks.*

**Tom**   You were the first in your family to go to university, right?

**Shelley**   And probably the last.

**Tom**   I bet they were proud of you. In fact I know they were.

*He goes to a sideboard and takes down a picture of her on her graduation day. They look at it.*

**Shelley**   That's right. Uncle Len was there. But him and me mum didn't speak all day. Great day, that was.

**Shelley** *replaces the picture. Silence.*

**Tom**   Your family were proud. My father's still furious I hadn't the slightest interest in PPE at Oxford.

**Shelley**   I've seen things differently since I went to uni. It's a different way of seeing life.

**Tom**   It's why we do it. What we do. To open minds and hearts.

**Shelley**   And what do you do when it's too late and they're stuck in their ways?

**Tom**    You try and you keep trying.

**Shelley**    Well that's very noble of you Tom.

*Silence.*

**Tom**    Do you think your uncle's left you anything in his will?

**Shelley**    I don't know and I don't care. Really.

**Tom**    Really?

**Shelley**    My mum's ruined her life with bitterness. I won't be complicit in it.

**Tom**    But you already are, they're your family.

*Silence.*

**Shelley**    Uncle Len tried a bit with her for years. But once he first had the trouble with his prostate and Mum wouldn't change her tune he turned against her. Actively sided with Auntie Doreen. And actually I don't blame him for that. I'll never forget the day my mum rung me and told me there was a problem with Uncle Len down below. She was so flippant about it. We never thought it would get him.

**Tom**    Really?

*Silence.*

**Shelley**    I don't want to talk about it anymore. I won't be part of it Tom.

**Tom**    But imagine if your Uncle Len did leave you something?

*She thinks.*

**Tom**    Imagine it, a place of our own. You've got to admit, it's pretty gruelling living sandwiched between all those people.

**Shelley**    It's London. And what could we afford in London?

*Silence.*

**Tom**   You'd have that garden. I'd have somewhere of my own to write.

*Silence.*

**Shelley**   No, Tom. You left your family behind and I left mine behind. We don't owe anyone anything. We understand each other. It's why we work.

*She takes the wine from him. She has a sip and then kisses him.* **Pam** *enters.*

**Pam**   Get a room!

*She takes the tea towels, and cling film off of the food. She shouts at the top of her voice.*

**Pam**   I declare my spread is open!

**Tom** *doesn't go near the buffet and instead takes his wine back from* **Shelley**, *while she grabs some food.* **Ken** *enters and fills up his plate with food. One by one* **Doreen**, **Barry** *and* **Jackie** *come in. Everyone is quiet and no one says anything. They all have their eyes on* **Ken**. *It takes as long as it takes.*

**Pam**   Here, Tom have you ever had jellied eels?

**Tom**   No I don't think I have.

**Pam**   Well today's your day.

**Barry**   Watching him eat a bowl a jellied eels would be like watching Gillian McKeith attempt a Bush Tucker Trial.

**Tom**   Really?

**Barry**   I can't stand them mate. To me the jellied eel is the crocodile penis.

**Jackie**   Barry!

**Ken** *moves and everyone watches him. He simply goes to the buffet for more food. Silence.*

**Tom** *shakes his head and downs the rest of his wine.*

**Tom**   I often think money is the emptiest thing in the world.

**Ken**   Well I tell you what son I've had money and I've not had money. And having money's better.

**Tom**   But there's more to life than money?

**Barry**   If you're not bothered Tom, I'll have yours.

**Tom**   We've got a government of philistines. The price of everything and the value of nothing. What about the arts? Culture? The soul? If only we still had a Labour government.

*He fetches himself more wine.*

**Shelley**   Tom.

**Barry**   And what d'you think Labour would have done Brains of Britain? It's Labour that ruined everything.

**Ken**   They've left us a mountain of debt Tom.

**Barry**   I can't make a move now for the mob Blair and Brown let in. Undercutting me on jobs. They make the Polish look expensive. They'll work for virtually nothing. And if you open your mouth you're called a racist.

**Tom**   And what about the banks? It was the banks' fault/

**Ken**   I make you right. But Labour didn't do anything about them did they? I tell you I voted for Blair in '97 and again in 2001. But never again. I wouldn't vote Labour again. I've gone back to the Tories. At least you know where you stand.

**Barry**   They're all as bad as each other in my book Tom.

**Tom**   And what will the Tories do? We don't make anything in this country anymore.

**Ken** *reaches inside his pocket. Everyone focuses on him. He takes out his phone and looks at it before putting it away.*

**Doreen**   The old East End has changed so much. And Basildon's going the same way.

**Shelley**   Mum won't go into Romford now of an evening it's so full of yobs.

**Tom**   But what about other things?

**Barry**   What other things?

**Tom**   Art. Living a good life. Education.

**Barry**   You can have your art if you can pay for it.

**Pam**   I tell you what we want. Jobs. A decent health service. Not being frightened of getting old. We was always Labour in my house. Never again.

**Tom**   And you think the Tories will give you what you want?

**Barry**   And what did Labour ever do for us? Nothing's changed.

**Tom**   What about all the new schools and hospitals? They're demolishing the old flats you lived in and they've built you new ones.

**Barry**   That's because if they don't demolish them, they'll fucking fall down.

*Silence.*

**Shelley**   Tom's always had money. You've always had money, Tom. He feels guilty.

**Tom**   I don't.

**Shelley**   You do Tom. And there's nothing more unattractive than liberal guilt.

**Tom**   What you call liberal guilt darling, I call old-fashioned conscience.

*Silence.*

**Ken**   Barry likes to knock the foreigners but I don't find them at fault personally. In the last ten years there've been three million jobs created in this country but English white people think they're above taking them. Tebbit was right, they should get on their bike.

**Tom**   And what if you haven't got a bike?

**Ken**   You walk.

**Tom**   Wow.

**Ken**   You've got to get out and do a day's work. You've got to go on and get on and make your own luck.

**Tom**   But you do something you enjoy, you went out and met people, and worked with your hands?

**Ken**   It makes no difference. You've got to put bread on the table. And if I put bread on my table why should I put bread on another man's table when he's too fucking lazy to get off of his arse?

**Tom**   But.

**Ken**   But what son?

**Tom**   That's not fair.

**Ken**   Life's not fair.

**Tom**   But. What about compassion?

**Ken**   We all like to be generous. But sometimes son there's nothing left in the piggy bank.

**Barry**   None of us in this family have ever been on the dole. And when we're out of work, we look after each other. You've got to have some pride in yourself.

**Jackie**   I've been on the dole.

**Doreen**   They're all like that from Barking.

*Silence.*

**Jackie** *looks at* **Barry** *whose head goes down.*

**Jackie**   You can be a nasty so-and-so when you want to be Doreen.

**Doreen**   I know darling.

**Jackie** *leaves the room. Silence.*

**Ken** *looks at his watch.*

**Ken**   Where's your mother?

**Shelley**   Where is she Barry?

**Barry**   She was in the garden having a smoke.

*Silence.*

**Tom**   Surely you agree there's more to life than looking after yourself and your immediate family?

**Shelley**   Tom, go and find Mum.

**Tom** *ignores her.*

**Doreen**   And who's ever cared about us?

*Silence.*

**Ken**   That's right.

**Ken** *and* **Doreen** *look at each other. She turns away.*

**Tom**   But where's the hope? Where's the future?

*Silence.*

**Jackie** *comes back in.*

**Tom**   But surely you agree education's important?

**Shelley**   Don't start something you can't finish Tom.

**Tom**   Look at Shelley. She went to university. We're teachers.

**Jackie**   And you've certainly gone up in the world haven't you doll? All the way to Walthamstow. I am jealous.

**Shelley**   Jackie?

**Barry**   Oi.

**Doreen** *looks at her watch and then looks at* **Ken**. *Silence.*

**Barry**   I was booted out of school and I come right in the end.

**Tom**    But you had Lenny? Not everyone has a Lenny –

**Doreen**    People like us have never been too bothered about things like that. We're not like people like you Tom. We're right proud of Shelley.

*She scowls at* **Jackie** *and smiles at* **Shelley** *before focusing on* **Tom**.

**Doreen**    But all's the same we're entitled to our views.

**Tom** *paces and loses his rag a bit.*

**Tom**    But this is ridiculous! Listen to yourselves! This is just simple-minded ignorance!

*Silence.*

**Barry**    I think you wanna put a cork in it before you start upsetting anyone.

**Shelley**    Empathy Tom, empathy.

**Tom**    No one likes a smart arse.

**Barry**    If you fucking open that mouth again I'll fucking shut it for you. All right?

**Ken** *coughs. They all look at him. Silence.*

**Ken**    You see the trouble with the lefty type is he's always open-minded and all that jazz until someone disagrees with him. You won't get anywhere son until you try and think about what it's like standing in our shoes.

*Silence.*

England's a Conservative country.

**Tom**    Labour and the Lib Dems got nearly five million votes more than the Tories at the last election. How does that make Britain Conservative? The worst recession since the 1930s and the Tories still couldn't win.

**Ken**    I'm talking about England son.

**Tom**    I think you're talking about Essex. I think you're being myopic actually.

**Shelley**  Tom, be quiet now, please.

**Ken**  And who doesn't look in their own back yard?

**Tom**  Look, Ken –

**Ken**  And how many never even bothered to vote, answer that one?

**Barry**  I didn't.

**Tom**  Well that's just apathy.

**Ken**  That's right son, that's exactly what it is. And why do you think we feel apathetic? They're going to squeeze us until the fucking pips squeak son. And what have we done to deserve that when all we've done is graft?

*Silence.*

You've no right to judge son. You've never known what it's like to have no money. A little bird tells me you're not speaking to your old man. But I bet your allowance plops in the old bank account on the first of every month doesn't it son?

*Silence.*

When my wife was first diagnosed with breast cancer things weren't so good with the business. We had the eighties boom and then there was the bust. Money was tight. For a month when there was absolutely nothing, no money at all, I walked six mile and back to visit her in hospital rather than waste a train fare. I'm sorry but you've no fucking idea son. You've no right to sit in judgement over us.

*Silence.*

**Maureen** *enters and helps herself to the buffet. She notices everyone looking at her.*

**Maureen**  Don't mind me.

*Silence.*

**Ken**  Anyway. Now Maureen's here.

*He coughs loudly to catch everyone's attention. Silence.*

We've business to attend to.

**Maureen**   That's right.

**Ken** *takes a sealed envelope from inside his jacket pocket and opens it with care. Silence.*

*He puts his glasses on. They are dirty. He cleans his glasses. He looks at the letter and reads the first half of the letter. He laughs.*

**Barry**   What is it? What's he done?

**Ken** *shakes his head and laughs.*

**Barry**   Well read it out then!

**Ken** *regains his composure and reads aloud.*

**Ken**   'To my family and my best mate Ken.'

**Barry**   And?

**Ken**   'You will all know by now that two months ago I changed my will and in due course all the proper processes will unfold. My solicitor Mr Grey remains my sole executor. Many of you will know, or have heard that I had left my house –.'

**Maureen**   It was never his house.

**Doreen**   Quiet.

*Silence.*

**Ken**   'I had left my house to Barry. There were various small bequests but I had basically left everything to Barry. On reflection I think I did the wrong thing.'

**Jackie** *wipes her eyes and* **Barry** *tries to comfort her. Silence.*

**Ken**   'It was the first time I had the problem with my prostate. And Barry and Jackie were living a life of misery in their little flat. And I felt under a certain amount of pressure from you, Doreen.'

**Barry**   You made him didn't yer, you silly cow?

**Doreen**   I didn't make him do anything!

**Ken**   Be quiet both of you!

*Silence.*

'There have been certain things for what I wanted. A small private funeral. And I trust once this business is done the memorial service I'd like at Fords will happen. I know everything will have been done to a tee by my best mate Ken.'

*He becomes very moved.*

'You're a diamond Kenny.'

*He has to compose himself.*

**Doreen**   Get on with it.

**Ken** *looks at* **Doreen** *with pure hate. Silence.*

**Ken**   'The only thing wrong with you, mate, is you support Spurs but I live in hope. I bequest to you my season ticket.'

*He looks up and laughs.*

He's left me his season ticket.

*He wipes his eyes and goes on.*

**Ken**   'And to my family, I won't explain why I've done what I've done. It will only make things worse. But I hope what I've done puts a stop to the trouble. I should have done it donkey's years ago.'

*Silence.*

**Ken**   'The contents of the new will are as follows. The house is valued at two hundred and fifty grand and it is to be sold.'

**Doreen** *gasps and cries.*

**Doreen**   It's not right, this is my home.

*She sobs.*

**Ken**   'It won't fetch that. I expect it will be more like two hundred and twenty-five. Following on from the sale this is what I'd like to do with the proceeds. Barry and Shelley will each receive twenty-five thousand pounds. Plenty for a deposit for a property there. The contents of the house not belonging to Doreen will be divided equally between my sisters Doreen and Maureen. You have no say in who gets what. My executor has a detailed inventory. After my niece and nephew have had their money and my sisters have had their bequest. The following gifts should be made. Ten thousand pounds to Ken to spend on a holiday with a lady friend.'

*He laughs. No one else does.*

Ever been on a cruise Maureen?

**Maureen**   No, I haven't Ken.

**Doreen** *turns away.*

**Barry**   Stop fucking about Ken.

**Ken** *looks at the letter again.*

**Ken**   'And a further gift of five thousand pounds should be made to Pam next door.'

*Everyone looks at* **Pam**. *Silence.*

**Ken**   He goes on. 'After everything. After bills are paid and so on and so forth. I expect there'll be around one hundred and fifty thousand pounds left over. It is my instruction that all remaining monies are to be divided equally between Macmillan Cancer Support and the Prostate Cancer Charity.'

**Doreen**   He what?

**Ken**   He's given the money to charity darling.

**Maureen**   But he can't it's our money.

*The news sinks in. Silence.*

**Ken**   Well the house belongs to him and that's what he's done. He's given the lion's share away to charity.

**Doreen**    He's fucking given the money to charity! I fucking thought charity begun at home! You fucking prat Lenny! You soft fucking prat!

**Tom** *slows claps until* **Shelley** *stares at him. Silence.*

**Pam**    Five thousand pounds. Well I never. Five thousand pounds for little old me. God bless you Lenny.

**Doreen**    Whore.

*Silence.*

**Pam**    Now I know you're piqued but there's no need for that Dor.

**Doreen**    Piqued?

**Pam**    That's what I said. Cocked a deaf 'un have yer?

*She helps herself to a sausage roll from the spread.*

**Doreen**    Get out. Go on. Get out. Do one.

**Pam**    Dor.

**Doreen**    Don't you ever come near me or mine again. You've got what you were after.

**Pam**    I've what?

**Doreen**    And you can poke them tickets for Des O'Connor right up your arse while you're at it. Go on. Piss off. You can shit in your hat and punch it you fucking old trollop.

*Silence.*

**Barry**    Mum.

**Pam** *hesitates by the spread, picks up one of the large tubs of jellied eels, approaches* **Doreen** *and tips it over her head.*

**Pam**    And thanks a bunch for putting out the spread. Not.

*She throws the empty bowl against a wall and gestures with her middle finger, sucks it and gestures with it again.*

**Barry**    Go home Pam.

*She goes out. They watch her go and* **Doreen** *tries to wipe herself clean.*

**Shelley**   Is that it?

**Ken**   He's signed off 'Up the Hammers' and that's it.

*He places the letter in* **Doreen**'s *hand, goes to the spread and opens a can of Foster's which he swigs from.*

**Maureen**   So Doreen, he's left us with nothing.

**Shelley**   It's not nothing.

**Maureen**   You're all right you're rolling in it now.

**Shelley**   I don't want it.

*Silence.*

**Doreen**   By rights it's not yours anyway.

**Maureen**   It is hers.

**Doreen**   It's not.

**Maureen**   You did me out of my share and now you're trying to do my daughter out of hers.

**Shelley**   I told you I don't want it. I don't want to be part of it.

**Barry**   Shelley it's yours.

**Jackie**   It's not it's ours!

**Barry**   Jackie!

**Jackie**   It's ours! We was promised!

**Barry**   Jackie darling.

**Jackie**   We was promised!

**Barry**   Jackie, its twenty-five grand. There's plenty for a deposit for our own place.

**Jackie**   Even if we put down twenty-five grand how are we going to get a mortgage with your credit history Barry? And how are we going to get a mortgage with me working at Tesco's?

**Barry**  I'm the breadwinner darling –

**Jackie**  As far as the tax man's concerned you've only earned fifteen grand a year for the last three years! And do you think I'm that thick I haven't seen the letters from the VAT?

**Barry**  I'll sort it out.

**Ken**  Dear God, Barry –

**Jackie**  You won't. You've not changed Barry! You'll never change! We won't have nothing! Same as always! Nothing!

**Barry**  We will.

**Jackie**  We was gonna live here and I was gonna be a stay at home mum. Instead there's nothing but stress. Trying to make ends meet. Why do you think I can't get pregnant? Because there's nothing wrong with you or me is there? I produce more eggs than a fucking hen house.

*Silence.*

**Ken**  That's it. I've had it. Ta-ta all.

**Jackie** *wipes her eyes.* **Ken** *shakes his head and goes out.*

**Doreen**  You should go in with me Barry.

**Barry**  No, Mum.

**Doreen**  I've got fifty grand in policies and what not for my retirement.

**Barry**  No.

**Doreen**  We could buy a house together. It would be nice the three of us. And one day. If you do ever manage to get her pregnant then I'll be there. To look after it.

*Silence.*

**Jackie**  Nice? You make the Gorgonzola in *Jason and the Argonauts* look like a Cabbage Patch Kid. You'd fucking freeze the piss of the wicked witch of the east at a hundred paces. We want our own house!

**Doreen**   I've never had my own house why should you have one!

**Barry**   She's had a shock. She's upset.

**Doreen**   I don't want to be on my own. I don't want to be on my own. I want Lenny. Lenny! Lenny!

**Barry**   Bite your lip Mum.

**Doreen** *is shocked herself and nods.* **Jackie** *weeps.*

**Maureen**   Come on Shelley, Tom, get your coats.

*She makes to leave but* **Shelley** *is still, looking at* **Barry**.

**Barry**   I'm standing on my own two feet now.

**Maureen**   You sound like you're still having trouble crawling Barry.

*Silence.*

**Shelley**   You can have my money.

**Tom**   Shelley.

**Maureen**   Don't you dare!

**Barry**   No.

**Shelley**   Please Barry I don't want it.

**Maureen**   Now get your coat.

**Barry**   Fair's fair. You promised me Shell there wouldn't be no disagreement between us. There's never been a crossed word between us. Has there Shell? Please, it's your money. I won't take it.

**Shelley**   You will Barry.

**Barry**   I won't.

**Jackie** *composes yourself. Silence.*

**Doreen**   Where's your spine Barry?

**Tom**    Shelley, they're not entitled to it.

**Shelley** *looks at him.*

**Shelley**    No. I want you to take it.

**Barry**    No Shell.

**Shelley**    Take it.

**Barry**    No Shell.

**Shelley**    I said take it.

**Barry**    No Shell I won't.

*Silence.*

**Barry**    One day you'll resent it. You know you will. It's human nature.

**Shelley**    I won't Barry. I love you. You're the BFB. When I was seven I wanted you to take me away and marry me –

**Jackie**    Hark at her! Hark at her! We don't want your money anyway. I'd rather drink a litre of bleach.

**Barry**    Jackie.

**Jackie**    You won't shut me up this time Barry.

**Barry**    You'll do as you're told.

**Shelley**    Let her say her piece.

*Silence.*

**Jackie**    Once in a blue moon you come and see us, and you don't even take your coat off and sit down. You don't never have anything to eat when I offer it. You don't take no interest in anything me or Barry's got to say. We have to watch what you want on the telly when you come round. Or you switch it off. Our telly. In our home. And do you think I don't know what you said about me when Barry told yer we was getting married. And even when your Uncle Len was dying you never bothered to come and see him. Above

Basildon I expect. Waltzing about the place like your shit don't stink. You're a stuck up cunt, that's all you are and that's all you'll ever be.

**Shelley** *goes for* **Jackie** *and the family struggles to pull them apart. As* **Barry** *tries to pull* **Shelley** *off of* **Jackie**, **Shelley** *hits him very hard and he hits her back on reflex. She falls back, a dead weight. Silence.*

**Doreen** *is stunned.* **Jackie** *cries.* **Maureen** *and* **Tom** *go to* **Shelley**. **Jackie** *pulls* **Barry** *back.* **Tom** *goes to* **Shelley**.

**Tom**   She's out cold.

*Everyone looks at* **Barry** *except* **Tom** *who tries to bring her round.*

**Tom**   Shelley? Shelley –

**Barry**   Shelley! Shelley! Please!

**Tom**   It's okay she's coming round.

**Barry**   I'm sorry. I'm sorry, I'm sorry, I'm sorry.

**Tom** *sits* **Shelley** *up. Her nose is covered in blood and she cries.* **Maureen** *stands up and looks at* **Barry**.

**Maureen**   Well you've gone and done it now Barry. And I thought there wasn't nothing else much to break in this family. Your Uncle Len always said you'd end up in prison. And that's exactly where you're going.

*Silence.*

*Fade.*

## Act Four

*The same, except it's eighteen years earlier.*

*Mid-April 1992.*

*The dining table is back in its place. The furniture is the same, but some of the soft furnishings are different.*

**Len**, *who is 42, sits watching* **Shelley**, *who is 7, run around.*

**Len**  I can see you Shelley. I can see you.

*She runs towards him, and he picks her up and puts her on his knee. She whispers in his ear.*

**Len**  Where's Barry?

*She nods and whispers in his ear again.*

**Len**  The BFB? What's the BFB?

**Shelley**  The Big Friendly Barry.

*He laughs and thinks – sighs.*

**Len**  He's out darling. It's a Friday night. They're all out in Basildon.

**Maureen** *enters. She is 32.*

**Len**  All right Maur, I'm Hank Marvin here.

**Maureen**  Doreen won't be long.

**Len**  I hope she remembers my Wally.

**Maureen**  We need to talk Len.

**Len**  Is that why you're here?

**Maureen**  Yes, it is darling.

*Silence.*

**Len**  I'm tired.

**Maureen**  Why?

**Len**   I stayed up all night watching the election results come in.

**Maureen**   I never thought John Major would get back in.

*Silence.*

**Len**   And we had a pig of day today. Cor. I wish I'd stayed in bed and got some sleep.

**Maureen**   What's up Len?

**Len**   It's going to pot Dagenham ain't it? The sooner I get myself in the back office the better. Get myself a job up at Brentwood. The drive will be better that's for sure. I don't think there's ten thousand working for Fords in Dagenham now.

*Silence.*

**Len**   And there's rumours the Mondeo's going to Belgium. They're going to manufacture it over there.

*Silence.*

**Maureen**   I thought you went out for a drink with Ken on a Friday night.

**Len**   No, I was meant to be having a drink with that Pam next door.

**Shelley** *jumps off of* **Len**'s *knee and runs out.*

**Maureen**   Don't you get up to anything Shelley.

**Len**   Doreen don't like it does she.

**Maureen**   It's none of her business.

**Len**   Well Doreen's got a bit pally with Pam. Doreen's on her own. Pam's on her own.

**Maureen**   Is everyone in Basildon divorced?

*He laughs.*

**Maureen**   You should tell Doreen to keep her nose out.

**Len**   Well she don't like the idea of me knocking off her mate does she.

*Silence.*

**Maureen**   You shouldn't be on your own Len.

*Silence.*

**Len**   I'm all right.

**Maureen**   I know you'd love to meet someone. I know you'd love to have a family of your own.

**Len**   I told yer, I'm all right.

**Maureen**   You're too good Len.

**Len**   What?

**Maureen**   Sometimes in life you have to be cruel to be kind.

*Silence.*

**Len**   I was hoping me and Pam next door and Doreen and Ken could go out as a four.

**Maureen**   That sounds nice.

**Len**   Thought we could go for a carvery one Sunday lunchtime.

**Maureen**   Well why don't you go?

**Len**   Doreen don't like Ken does she.

**Maureen**   What's wrong with Ken?

**Len**   He's a diamond is Ken.

**Maureen**   What's wrong with him?

**Len**   She finds fault. She says she don't like it because he told her in conversation if he ever got married again he'd wear two wedding rings. He'd always have pictures of his wife up. She reckons she wants a clean slate the next time she meets a man.

**Maureen**   Well that's not going to happen is it, unless she starts going with some toy boy?

**Len**   That's another thing. She keeps moaning that he's old. I said Dor, you're not going to have any more kids. Ken's a bed of roses waiting to happen.

**Maureen**   She's always been headstrong has Doreen.

**Len**   The difficult middle child, I don't know.

*They both laugh.*

**Maureen**   Where's Barry?

**Len**   Out.

**Maureen**   Where?

**Len**   He goes to Raquels in Basildon. And then him and his mates go to this rave thing in Rainham, called Berwick Manor.

**Maureen**   Has he got himself a job yet?

**Len**   It'd be a start if he had an haircut. When was the last time you saw him Maur?

**Maureen**   Christmas.

*Silence.*

**Len**   He's decided to grow that bob of his out and his hair's on his shoulders now! He looks like a girl! I said to him, what's wrong with yer!

*She laughs.*

**Len**   He's turning into a right Alka-Seltzer in the arse-hole. If he's not careful he's gonna end up in prison.

*Silence.*

**Maureen**   Well where does he get his money?

**Len**   Where do you think? Bank of Len. And as for the rest don't ask. I said to him, Barry you've got a good apprenticeship on a plate there with Ken. You can get your City and Guilds and course Ken'll walk over water for

Doreen. You know, Barry's gonna get a good grounding with Ken. They won't listen to me. Neither of them. And Barry? All he wants to do is go out with his mates and pop them ecstasy pills.

*Silence.*

**Maureen**    Perhaps you shouldn't give him any more money?

**Len**    Yer, and he'd be gone like that.

*He clicks his fingers.*

And so would any chances he had in life.

*Silence.*

**Maureen**    Perhaps Doreen and Barry should get their own place?

**Len**    Where?

**Maureen**    Well they could go down the council?

**Len**    What?

**Maureen**    If they can't afford to buy nowhere then they'll have to live within their means.

**Len**    And what? Go and live on the tenth floor of some fucking shit-hole block of flats?

**Maureen**    Well –

**Len**    Mum and Dad come out of the East End to Romford. And then they come out here to Basildon after that. Because they wanted something better.

*Silence.*

**Maureen**    Well I don't know why she's turning her nose up at Ken.

**Len**    She doesn't like him.

**Maureen**    Why?

**Len**    She says he's got grey hairs.

**Maureen**    Well that's just a distinguished look.

**Len**    She doesn't want Ken because she wants what you've got. That's at the root of it.

*Silence.*

**Maureen**    And what's that?

**Len**    The perfect man. The perfect marriage. Don't you think she'd have liked to be a housewife? Do you think she wants to be on the till at Tesco's?

*Silence.*

**Maureen**    One day when you get married you'll realise there's no such thing as a perfect marriage.

**Len**    You've got money.

**Maureen**    We haven't got very much money anymore Len.

*Silence.*

**Len**    Well you've got a husband who stands by you. All Doreen had was a rat bag.

**Maureen**    You don't know what goes on behind closed doors Len.

**Len**    She's always been jealous.

*Silence.*

I give up with Barry. He didn't sit one GCSE. For three years he's sat on his arse. Where's his pride?

**Maureen**    He needs a father figure.

**Len**    Well –

**Maureen**    If Doreen would only look at Ken.

**Len**    She won't.

**Maureen**    I'll talk to her.

**Len**    It won't make no difference.

**Maureen**    I'm her sister.

**Len**  She won't listen.

**Maureen**  Women put things in different ways.

**Len**  You'll be pissing into the wind.

**Maureen**  What Barry needs is a job and a father figure. And Doreen has got Ken standing there on a plate.

**Len**  And what's wrong with me?

*Silence.*

**Maureen**  You're his uncle Len, you're not his dad.

**Len**  So this is all my fault is it?

*Silence.*

**Maureen**  No.

**Len**  The only reason your sister and your nephew have got shoes on their feet is because of me.

**Maureen**  I make you right Len.

*Silence.*

**Len**  Well what then?

**Maureen**  I think you should never have come to Romford with Mum and Dad.

*Silence.*

**Len**  Why?

**Maureen**  You was older. You had a job.

**Len**  I was twenty years of age.

**Maureen**  You had your own life.

**Len**  I was a grease monkey in a tuppeney ha'penny garage in Kenton Road.

**Maureen**  But you had your mates. You had a girlfriend.

**Len**  I wanted to go and work in Fords.

**Maureen**    And in ten years Fords in Dagenham will be gone. I guarantee it.

**Len**    Thanks Maur, rub it in a little bit more.

*He shakes his head, gets up and walks away from the table.*

**Maureen**    I will say something about Barry.

**Len**    What?

**Maureen**    You spoil him Len.

**Len**    Turn it in. He has a little bit of pocket money and that's it.

*Silence.*

**Len**    So what if I treat him.

**Maureen**    Treat him? He goes out in new Kickers. He's got them Wallabees in about six different colours. He wears Naf Naf and Chippie. I know what that costs.

**Len**    Why shouldn't he have nice things?

**Maureen**    I'm not saying that –

**Len**    Why shouldn't he have a nice roof over his head?

**Maureen**    I'm not –

**Len**    Mum and Dad put everything into moving out to Romford. And then doing it all again to come out to Basildon. So we had something better and our children had something better.

**Maureen**    But he's not your son Len.

**Len**    I know he's not!

*Silence.*

**Maureen**    I don't think you'd spoil your own boy like it.

*There's noise.* **Doreen**, *who is 37, enters with fish and chips wrapped in newspaper.*

**Doreen**    Hello Maureen.

**Maureen**    Hello Doreen.

*She goes to **Maureen** and they kiss and **Doreen** puts the takeaway on the table and they sort it out and begin to eat.*

**Maureen**    I haven't seen fish and chips wrapped in paper for ages.

**Len**    You don't see it now do you?

**Maureen**    Here Dor, I've tried that pie and mash in Romford.

**Doreen**    What's it like?

**Maureen**    It's not a patch on Kelly's in Roman Road.

**Doreen**    We'll have to go.

**Maureen**    Well we said we'd go and see Aunt Rose.

**Doreen**    We can go up together. Perhaps we can get on the tube at Mile End after and go up West? I haven't been to Selfridges in years.

**Len**    You haven't got Selfridges money.

**Doreen**    I want to look.

**Maureen**    That'd be nice doll.

**Doreen**    That would be nice doll.

**Maureen**    We don't see enough of each other.

**Doreen**    We don't darling.

**Maureen**    I miss you Doreen.

**Doreen**    I know, I miss you darling.

**Maureen**    Shelley! Your dinner's here! Auntie Doreen wants to see you!

**Doreen**    I love yer Maur.

**Maureen**    I love yer Dor.

**Doreen**  I love your bones.

**Maureen**  I love you more.

**Len**  I always get left out.

*The three siblings laugh.* **Shelley** *skips in and onto her mum's knee where they share the chips.*

**Len**  You didn't get my Wally did yer?

**Doreen**  Sugar.

**Shelley** *whispers in* **Maureen***'s ear.*

**Maureen**  Ah she wants to know where Barry is?

**Doreen**  Ah she worships my Barry.

**Len**  I told yer Shelley, Barry's out.

**Maureen** *stops eating and thinks.*

**Maureen**  Is it all right if we talk?

**Doreen**  I'm all ears Maur.

*Silence.*

**Maureen**  It's been ten years since Dad died.

**Doreen**  Innit a tragedy he hardly got to enjoy this house?

**Maureen**  And it's been five since Mum died and she left the house to you Len.

*Silence.*

**Shelley** *jumps down and runs around the room.*

**Maureen**  Stop it Shelley.

**Shelley** *pokes her tongue out at her mum and runs off.*

**Len**  Well don't stand on ceremony, spit it out Maur.

**Maureen**  I know Mum was old-fashioned and left it to the eldest son.

**Doreen**  Well Len has been paying the mortgage since Dad died.

**Maureen**  I know.

*Silence.*

**Doreen**  Well what is it Maur?

**Maureen**  You said to me and Doreen when Mum died and she left you the house that it wasn't right.

*Silence.*

**Maureen**  You said it was old-fashioned.

**Len**  That's right.

**Maureen**  You said by rights this house belonged to the three of us.

**Len**  Yer?

**Maureen**  You said.

**Len**  Go on.

**Maureen**  You said if me or Doreen ever needed the money you'd sell this house and after the mortgage was paid down we could split it three ways.

*Silence.*

**Len**  Yes, I did Maureen.

*Silence.*

**Maureen**  My circumstances have changed.

**Doreen** *and* **Len** *stop eating. Silence.*

**Len**  What's happened?

**Maureen**  Martin's been hanging on in his firm by his fingernails for years.

**Len**  What?

**Maureen**  He just about hung on to his job after Black Monday. But not anymore.

*Silence.*

**Len**   When did he lose his job?

**Maureen**   He lost it in the New Year. It's why we haven't been near nor by.

*She takes a tissue and wipes her eyes.*

**Len**   Well Doreen's here now with Barry.

**Maureen**   I know.

*Silence.*

**Doreen**   I'm sorry Maureen. I feel awful.

**Maureen**   It's not your fault.

*Silence.*

**Doreen**   Well we've got to get it sorted out haven't we?

**Maureen**   We've got a whacking great mortgage. We're going to lose everything.

**Len**   I told you, you was stretching yourself buying that big house in Gidea Park.

**Doreen**   Now's not the time for recrimination Len.

**Maureen**   I've been so worried.

**Doreen**   What about?

**Maureen**   That you'd be angry.

**Doreen**   Why?

**Maureen**   Because you've been living here with Barry.

**Doreen**   No, darling.

**Maureen**   Are you sure?

**Doreen**   You're my sister.

**Maureen**   Thank you Doreen, it means so much darling. Thank you. I'm so grateful I can't tell yer.

*She wipes her eyes. Silence.*

**Doreen**  You listen to your big sister Maureen. We grew up the three of us standing by and watching our mum fall out with her sisters one by one. You was still a baby but I remember mum going toe to toe with Aunt Rose on the cobbles down Roman Road over two bob. We're not going to do things like that are we darling?

**Maureen**  No.

*Silence.*

We've been so hard up.

**Len**  Hard up?

**Maureen**  We've been selling everything.

**Len**  Has he still got that Porsche?

**Doreen** *tuts.*

**Maureen**  That went right away.

**Doreen**  You can be right insensitive at times Len.

**Len**  What have I said?

**Doreen**  If there was a great big pile of shit right in front of your face you'd still walk in it.

**Len**  What?

**Maureen**  And Martin's turned.

**Len**  What?

**Maureen**  He's been drinking and we've been arguing. I don't know him anymore.

**Len**  What?

**Maureen**  He's acting like a madman. And that's not the half of it.

*She wipes her eyes.*

**Len**  Has he hurt you?

**Maureen**  No.

**Len**    Has he laid a finger on you?

**Maureen**    Len –

**Len**    I'll fucking kill him! I'll fucking strangle the cunt! I'll kill him!

**Doreen**    Len!

**Len**    I will!

**Doreen**    Shelley's here.

**Len** *paces the room. He looks at* **Maureen**.

**Doreen**    I'm coming over to see you on Sunday. Len'll give us a lift won't you Len?

**Len** *nods*.

**Maureen**    Will you?

**Doreen**    I'll bring some shopping with me.

**Maureen**    No –

**Doreen**    It won't cost me anything at the end of a Saturday. Not with my staff discount as well. And as for your husband? He can have long hard look at our Lenny's ugly mug and have a think about whether he fancies having his features rearranged Basildon style.

**Maureen** *laughs and then cries a bit*.

**Maureen**    I'm so embarrassed. I've never been so embarrassed in all my life.

**Doreen**    What for?

**Maureen**    We had so much money.

*Silence*.

**Doreen**    Don't think about that now darling.

**Maureen**    It makes me sick to think about it.

**Doreen**    Don't you be embarrassed you're with your brother and your sister.

**Maureen**   I always dreamed my Shelley would go to university when she grows up. She was going to be the first in our family to go. I've dreamed about it. I can't tell yer. In her gown.

*She wipes her eyes.*

**Len**   She will. My niece and my nephew will never go without.

*Silence.*

**Maureen**   Yer, she will. I'll do anything to make sure she gets there.

**Doreen**   That's right.

**Len**   Don't you worry Maur we won't let you down.

*Silence.*

**Doreen**   We'll sell this house. Won't we Len?

**Len**   Yer.

*Silence.*

I know an estate agent in Laindon. He goes in The Castle Mayne.

**Maureen**   Will you talk to him?

**Len**   Yer.

**Doreen**   We'll get it sold.

**Len**   That's right.

**Doreen**   As soon as I get somewhere sorted out for me and Barry.

*Silence.*

**Len**   I promise you Maur. If I dropped down dead this house would pass to you and Doreen. It's in my will.

*Silence.*

**Maureen**   Will you both do this for me?

**Len**    I promise you.

**Maureen** *weeps with joy and relief and opens her arms.* **Len** *and* **Doreen** *go to her. The siblings, laughing and cuddling each other, make a touching picture.*

**Shelley** *enters wearing* **Len**'s *West Ham scarf.* **Len** *spots her.*

**Len**    What you been up to?

**Shelley** *giggles and runs to* **Doreen** *who puts her on her knee.*

**Doreen**    I'm surprised you're still awake. He was up half the night last night watching the election. He woke me up cheering.

**Len**    Do you know what that was?

**Maureen**    What?

**Len**    When we won in Basildon I knew we'd stuffed Kinnock. If that mob can't beat us in the worst recession since the 1930s I don't think Labour'll ever win again.

*Silence.*

**Maureen**    You never know what's going to happen Len.

**Len**    No chance.

*He smiles.*

I was telling Maur you've got my mate Ken knocking on your door.

**Doreen**    Don't.

**Maureen** *laughs.*

**Len**    He's on heat.

**Doreen**    It'd be like going on a date with Max Bygraves.

**Len**    He's a diamond is Ken.

*They all think. Silence.*

**Maureen**    How did you and Ken become mates?

**Len**   When we first moved here I was a bit hard up so I knocked on some doors and put a card up in the paper shop. Trying to drum up a bit of extra work fixing up some cars. Ken wanted me to look at his wife's Fiesta. We had a bit of a laugh about the football and that was it.

**Maureen**   Why don't you let him take you out Dor?

**Doreen** *laughs.*

**Doreen**   No.

**Maureen**   Why not?

**Doreen**   It don't feel right.

**Len**   He's got a good little business though ain't he?

**Doreen**   There's no spark there.

*Silence.*

**Len**   That sort of romantic thinking won't bring you nothing but heartache Dor.

**Maureen**   Says him, who can't keep the company of a woman for five minutes without finding fault with her.

**Len**   I've got high standards.

*They all laugh.*

**Maureen**   I think selling this house will be good.

*They all think. Silence.*

**Len**   It's funny timing all this talk about selling the house.

**Doreen**   Why?

*Silence.*

**Len**   They want someone who knows about the robots. That spray paint the body shell to go to Genk.

**Doreen**   To Genk?

**Len**   It's in Belgium. We've got a plant there. There's rumours they're going to make the Mondeo there.

*Silence.*

I've been thinking about it.

*Silence.*

Perhaps it's for the best I go.

**Maureen**    Do you want to go?

**Len**    I'm a bit nervous.

**Maureen**    Why?

**Len**    Of flying. I've never been abroad.

**Maureen**    You've been abroad?

**Doreen**    No he hasn't.

*Silence.*

Are you going Len?

**Len**    I wasn't going to but.

*Silence.*

**Maureen**    Why not?

**Len**    I don't know. Many's the time I've dreamed about it. Sometimes I think to myself, Len son, you've never been out of London or Essex, book a ticket, pack your bags and keep your fingers crossed the plane don't crash.

*Silence.*

I'd love to go to the Big Apple. I'd love that. The Empire State. The World Trade Center. The Statue of Liberty. Catch a Broadway show.

*Silence.*

**Len**    I'd go in the run-up to Christmas. Perhaps I'd fetch a present or two. A long coat for you Dor. And some shoes for you Maur. Some trainers for Barry. And a right nice dolly for Shelley.

**Maureen** *smiles.*

**Len**   It'd be Christmas. And the snow would be falling. And there I'd be in Times Square with a fucking beautiful sort on my arm. Blonde hair. Legs that go on for ever. And one of those velvety voices in the black and white pictures. The snow would be falling and I'd be whistling. 'I'm Forever Blowing Bubbles.'

**Maureen** *laughs*.

**Len**   I'd be grinning like a Cheshire Cat. And I'd shout out, 'I'm here New York! I'm here! Lenny's made it! I'm here!'

*Silence.*

**Doreen**   You're not going to leave us are you Len?

*Silence.*

Barry would be heart-broken.

*Silence.*

**Maureen**   But if the house is being sold –

**Doreen**   I know it is. But.

*Silence.*

**Len**   Don't upset yourself Dor. I've not made me mind up.

**Doreen**   Don't leave me Lenny.

*Silence.*

**Maureen**   Shelley!

**Len** *looks at his sisters, who are looking at each other.*

**Len**   We've got Norwich at home tomorrow.

**Maureen**   Shelley.

**Shelley** *runs to* **Maureen** *who holds her hand.*

**Len**   It was a shambles last week at Stamford Bridge. Cascarino ran riot. Billy Bonds kept them all locked in the away dressing room after for an inquisition.

*Silence.*

**Maureen**   So I'll see you on Sunday then?

*Silence.*

**Maureen**   Thank you.

*Silence.*

**Len**   I think we'll get a result against the Canaries.

**Maureen**   I mean it Len. I mean it Doreen. Thank you.

**Len**   Don't worry Maur.

*Silence.*

**Maureen**   Are you sure? You'll do it for me? You'll sell up? You won't change your mind?

**Doreen** *snaps at* **Maureen**.

**Doreen**   He give his word and that's the end of it.

*Silence.*

**Len**   Dor?

*Silence.*

**Doreen**   She had everything she wanted Len. And more.

**Maureen**   Let's not fall out over money Dor.

*Silence.*

You won't be on your own Doreen.

**Doreen**   Won't I?

**Maureen**   No, you've got me.

**Doreen**   Thank you darling.

**Maureen**   No, thank you darling.

**Len** *breaks out into a big smile.* **Doreen** *and* **Maureen** *look at each other. Silence.*

**Maureen**   I'm sad.

**Len**   What for?

**Maureen**  The house is going to be sold.

*Silence.*

**Len**  I thought I'd die in this house.

**Maureen**  Did you?

*Silence.*

**Doreen**  And instead you're going to Belgium.

*She walks away.*

**Maureen**  Doreen?

**Doreen**  Yes, Maureen?

**Maureen**  I'll wait to hear from you and Lenny then?

*The siblings continue looking at each other.*

*Fade.*

*The end.*

# Methuen Drama Modern Plays

*include work by*

Edward Albee
Jean Anouilh
John Arden
Margaretta D'Arcy
Peter Barnes
Sebastian Barry
Brendan Behan
Dermot Bolger
Edward Bond
Bertolt Brecht
Howard Brenton
Anthony Burgess
Simon Burke
Jim Cartwright
Caryl Churchill
Complicite
Noël Coward
Lucinda Coxon
Sarah Daniels
Nick Darke
Nick Dear
Shelagh Delaney
David Edgar
David Eldridge
Dario Fo
Michael Frayn
John Godber
Paul Godfrey
David Greig
John Guare
Peter Handke
David Harrower
Jonathan Harvey
Iain Heggie
Declan Hughes
Terry Johnson
Sarah Kane
Charlotte Keatley
Barrie Keeffe

Howard Korder
Robert Lepage
Doug Lucie
Martin McDonagh
John McGrath
Terrence McNally
David Mamet
Patrick Marber
Arthur Miller
Mtwa, Ngema & Simon
Tom Murphy
Phyllis Nagy
Peter Nichols
Sean O'Brien
Joseph O'Connor
Joe Orton
Louise Page
Joe Penhall
Luigi Pirandello
Stephen Poliakoff
Franca Rame
Mark Ravenhill
Philip Ridley
Reginald Rose
Willy Russell
Jean-Paul Sartre
Sam Shepard
Wole Soyinka
Simon Stephens
Shelagh Stephenson
Peter Straughan
C. P. Taylor
Theatre Workshop
Sue Townsend
Judy Upton
Timberlake Wertenbaker
Roy Williams
Snoo Wilson
Victoria Wood

# Methuen Drama Contemporary Dramatists

*include*

John Arden (two volumes)
Arden & D'Arcy
Peter Barnes (three volumes)
Sebastian Barry
Dermot Bolger
Edward Bond (eight volumes)
Howard Brenton
    (two volumes)
Richard Cameron
Jim Cartwright
Caryl Churchill (two volumes)
Sarah Daniels (two volumes)
Nick Darke
David Edgar (three volumes)
David Eldridge
Ben Elton
Dario Fo (two volumes)
Michael Frayn (three volumes)
David Greig
John Godber (four volumes)
Paul Godfrey
John Guare
Lee Hall (two volumes)
Peter Handke
Jonathan Harvey
    (two volumes)
Declan Hughes
Terry Johnson (three volumes)
Sarah Kane
Barrie Keeffe
Bernard-Marie Koltès
    (two volumes)
Franz Xaver Kroetz
David Lan
Bryony Lavery
Deborah Levy
Doug Lucie

David Mamet (four volumes)
Martin McDonagh
Duncan McLean
Anthony Minghella
    (two volumes)
Tom Murphy (six volumes)
Phyllis Nagy
Anthony Neilsen (two volumes)
Philip Osment
Gary Owen
Louise Page
Stewart Parker (two volumes)
Joe Penhall (two volumes)
Stephen Poliakoff
    (three volumes)
David Rabe (two volumes)
Mark Ravenhill (two volumes)
Christina Reid
Philip Ridley
Willy Russell
Eric-Emmanuel Schmitt
Ntozake Shange
Sam Shepard (two volumes)
Wole Soyinka (two volumes)
Simon Stephens (two volumes)
Shelagh Stephenson
David Storey (three volumes)
Sue Townsend
Judy Upton
Michel Vinaver
    (two volumes)
Arnold Wesker (two volumes)
Michael Wilcox
Roy Williams (three volumes)
Snoo Wilson (two volumes)
David Wood (two volumes)
Victoria Wood

For a complete catalogue
of Methuen Drama titles
write to:

Methuen Drama
Bloomsbury Publishing Plc
50 Bedford Square
London WC1B 3DP

or you can visit our website at:

www.methuendrama.com